D1922798

SECOND EDITION

face2face

Elementary Workbook with Key

Chris Redston with Gillie Cunningham

CAMBRIDGE UNIVERSITY PRESS

Contents

Introducing yourself REAL WORLD 0.1
Saying goodbye REAL WORLD 0.4

1 Fill in the gaps with these words.

~~Hello~~	Hi	I'm	my	meet	too	Nice

EDUARDO [1] *Hello* , [2] ______ name's Eduardo.
CHIARA [3] ______ , [4] ______ Chiara.
EDUARDO [5] ______ to [6] ______ you.
CHIARA You [7] ______ .

Goodbye	you	Bye	See	Monday

TEACHER [8] ______ , Toshi. [9] ______ you on [10] ______ .
TOSHI Yes, see [11] ______ . [12] ______ !

Numbers 0–20 VOCABULARY 0.1

2 Write the missing letters.

0 z *e* r *o*
1 o __ e
2 t __ o
3 th __ e __
4 f __ __ r
5 f __ v __
6 si __
7 s __ v __ __
8 ei __ __ t
9 n __ __ e
10 t __ n
11 e __ __ ve __
12 t __ el __ __
13 th __ __ t __ __ n
14 f __ __ r __ ee __
15 f __ __ t __ e __
16 s __ __ t __ en
17 s __ ve __ __ e __ n
18 ei __ __ t __ __ n
19 n __ __ e __ __ en
20 t __ __ n __ y

Classroom instructions REAL WORLD 0.2

3 Match the verbs in A to the words/phrases in B.

A	B
1 Compare	and practise.
2 Look	and answer the questions.
3 Listen	answers.
4 Work	exercise 3 on your own.
5 Ask	at the board.
6 Do	in groups.
7 Fill in	in pairs.
8 Listen	your book.
9 Open	and check.
10 Look	the words to the pictures.
11 Work	the gaps.
12 Match	at the photo on page 17.

The alphabet VOCABULARY 0.2

4 **a** Fill in the gaps. Use capital letters.

A *B* C *D* __ F __ H __ __ K __ __
N __ __ Q __ __ T __ V __ __ Y __

b Write the alphabet. Use small letters.

a b c ______

Things in the classroom VOCABULARY 0.3

5 Write the missing letters.

1 a T *V*

2 a c_ _ _ _

3 a D_ _ p_ _ _ _ _ _

4 a p_ _

5 a c_ _ _ _ _ _ _

6 a b_ _ _

7 a t_ _ _ _

8 a d_ _ _ _ _ _ _ _ _

9 a C_ p_ _ _ _ _

10 a p_ _ _ _ _

Names REAL WORLD 0.3

6 Fill in the gaps with these words.

~~What's~~	surname	Welcome	It's	
How	first	Thank	spell	class

TEACHER 1 *What's* your 2 ______ name, please?
DANIELA 3 ______ Daniela.
TEACHER What's your 4 ______ ?
DANIELA Iguarte.
TEACHER 5 ______ do you 6 ______ that?
DANIELA I-G-U-A-R-T-E.
TEACHER 7 ______ to the 8 ______ , Daniela.
DANIELA 9 ______ you.

Days of the week VOCABULARY 0.4

7 Write the days.

November

1 M *o n d a y*		6	13	20	27
2 T_ _ _ _ _ _ _		7	14	21	28
3 W_ _ _ _ _ _ _ _ _	1	8	15	22	29
4 T_ _ _ _ _ _ _	2	9	16	23	30
5 F_ _ _ _ _	3	10	17	24	
6 S_ _ _ _ _ _ _	4	11	18	25	
7 S_ _ _ _ _	5	12	19	26	

Introducing people REAL WORLD 1.1

1 Fill in the gaps with these phrases.

~~Hello~~ thanks You too I'm fine How are you this is Nice to meet you

DANIEL [1] *Hello*, Carlos.
CARLOS Hi, Daniel. [2] ______ ?
DANIEL [3] ______ , thanks. And you?
CARLOS I'm OK, [4] ______ .
DANIEL Carlos, [5] ______ Emma.
CARLOS Hello, Emma. [6] ______ .
EMMA [7] ______ .

Countries and nationalities VOCABULARY 1.1

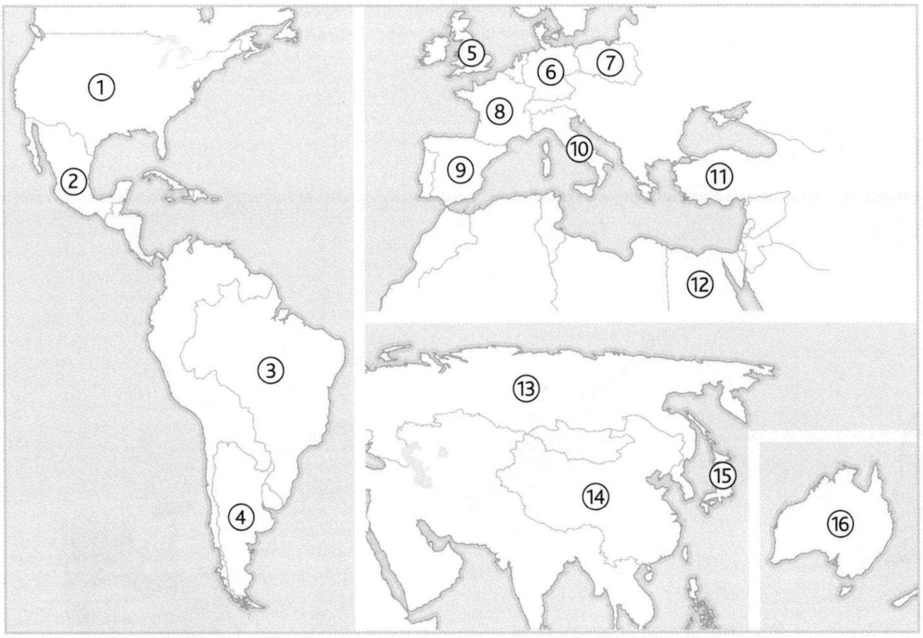

2 Look at the maps. Write the countries.

1 the *U S A*
2 M_ _ _ _ _
3 B_ _ _ _ _
4 A_ _ _ _ _ _ _ _
5 the _ _
6 G_ _ _ _ _ _
7 P_ _ _ _ _
8 F_ _ _ _ _
9 S_ _ _ _
10 I_ _ _ _
11 T_ _ _ _ _
12 E_ _ _ _
13 R_ _ _ _ _
14 C_ _ _ _
15 J_ _ _ _
16 A_ _ _ _ _ _ _ _

3 Write the nationalities for the countries in **2**.

1 A*m e r i c a n*
2 M_ _ _ _ _ _
3 B_ _ _ _ _ _ _ _
4 A_ _ _ _ _ _ _ _ _ _
5 B_ _ _ _ _ _
6 G_ _ _ _ _
7 P_ _ _ _ _
8 F_ _ _ _ _
9 S_ _ _ _ _ _
10 I_ _ _ _ _ _ _
11 T_ _ _ _ _ _
12 E_ _ _ _ _ _ _
13 R_ _ _ _ _ _
14 C_ _ _ _ _ _
15 J_ _ _ _ _ _ _
16 A_ _ _ _ _ _ _ _ _ _

be (1): positive and *Wh-* questions GRAMMAR 1.1

4 Write these sentences with contractions (*I'm*, *you're*, etc.).

1 I am from England.
I'm from England.
2 You are in room 403.
______
3 He is American.
______
4 We are from Istanbul.
______
5 She is a teacher.
______
6 They are Italian.
______
7 It is in room C.
______

5 Fill in the gaps with these words/phrases.

~~What's~~	from	name	Where	I'm

RECEPTIONIST [1] *What's* your [2]__________, please?
MEHMET It's Mehmet Demir.
RECEPTIONIST [3]__________ are you [4]__________?
MEHMET [5]__________ from Turkey.

We're	are you	What are	Our names

RECEPTIONIST [6]__________ your names, please?
ALEXANDER [7]__________ are Alexander and Lena Schneider.
RECEPTIONIST Where [8]__________ from?
ALEXANDER [9]__________ from Stuttgart, in Germany.

What are	They're	Where are	His name's	her name's

EDWARD [10]__________ their names?
RACHEL [11]__________ Tom and [12]__________ Elizabeth.
EDWARD [13]__________ they from?
RACHEL [14]__________ Australian.

Subject pronouns and possessive adjectives GRAMMAR 1.2

6 Choose the correct words.

1 *I*/(*My*) name is Andrew Wells.
2 *I/My* 'm from the USA.
3 What's *he/his* nationality?
4 Where are *they/their* from?
5 *She/Her* name's Patricia.
6 What are *they/their* names?
7 *He/His* 's a Spanish teacher.
8 It's *you/your* dictionary.
9 Where's *she/her* from?
10 *We/Our* 're English students.
11 Where's *you/your* teacher from?
12 This is *we/our* hotel.
13 *It's/Its* a CD player.
14 What's *she/her* nationality?

1B Coffee break

Jobs VOCABULARY 1.2

1 Do the puzzle. Find the job (↓).

1

2

6

7

3

4

8

9

5
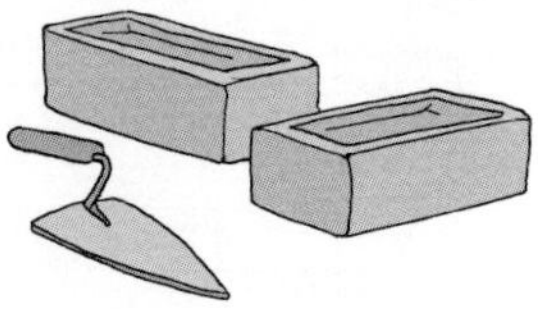

10
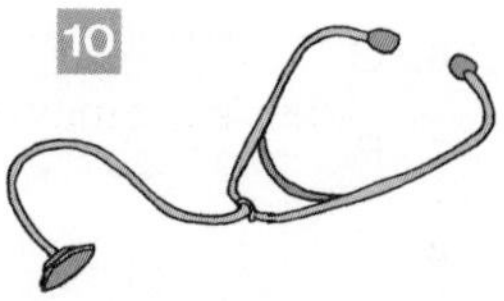

								↓								
1							L	A	W	Y	E	R				
2				P			I			O				C		R
3					T						R					
4					A				R							
5							B				D					
6	M				C											
7					W				R			S				
8			S				S			S			T			T
9				C						R						
10					D				O							

a and *an* VOCABULARY 1.3

2 Fill in the gaps with *a* or *an*.

1 *a* dentist
2 ______ English dictionary
3 ______ number
4 ______ actress
5 ______ housewife
6 ______ manager
7 ______ Australian hotel
8 ______ DVD player
9 ______ Italian teacher
10 ______ university

be (2): negative, *yes/no* questions and short answers

GRAMMAR 1.3

3 Make these sentences negative. Write two negative sentences if possible.

1 He's a doctor.
He isn't a doctor.
He's not a doctor.
2 We're from Poland.
______
______
3 You're late.
______
______
4 I'm retired.
______
______
5 They're from Rome.
______
______
6 She's an accountant.
______
______
7 Mark is unemployed.
______
______

Eric Clapton
musician (England)

Penélope Cruz
actress (Spain)

George Clooney and Brad Pitt actors (USA)

4 **a** Make questions with these words.

1 actor / Eric Clapton / an / Is ?
Is Eric Clapton an actor?
2 Is / actress / an / Penélope Cruz ?
______
3 musicians / and Brad Pitt / Are / George Clooney ?
______
4 from / Eric Clapton / England / Is ?
______
5 and Brad Pitt / from / George Clooney / Are / the USA ?
______
6 Penélope Cruz / Italy / Is / from ?
______

b Look at the pictures. Write short answers to the questions in **4a**.

1 *No, he isn't.* 3 ______ 5 ______
2 ______ 4 ______ 6 ______

Review

5 Fill in the gaps in these conversations.

A [1] *Are* you from England?
B No, I'm [2] ______ . I'm [3] ______ Australia.
A Oh, really? What's your [4] ______ ?
B I'm [5] ______ teacher.
A Are you [6] ______ English teacher?
B Yes, I [7] ______ .

A Excuse [8] ______ . Are you from Spain?
B [9] ______ , we aren't. We're [10] ______ Argentina.
A And what do you [11] ______ ?
B I'm [12] ______ lawyer and Luis is [13] ______ engineer.

Personal details

Numbers 20–100 VOCABULARY 1.4

1 Write the numbers.

a 22 t*wenty* -t*wo*
b 33 t______ -t______
c 44 f______ -f______
d 55 f______ -f______
e 66 s______ -s______
f 77 s______ -s______
g 88 e______ -e______
h 99 n______ -n______
i 100 a h______

2 Write the answers in words.

1 ten + seven – four = *thirteen*
2 nine + twenty-two = ______
3 eighty-six – fourteen = ______
4 thirteen + fifty-four = ______
5 ninety-eight – seventy = ______
6 twenty-three + eleven = ______
7 seventy – seventeen = ______
8 thirty-seven + sixty-three = ______

Asking for personal details REAL WORLD 1.2

3 **a** Read conversations 1–3. Fill in gaps a–j with the correct questions.

1 A OK, first I need your personal details. [a] *What's your surname?*
B It's King.
A [b] ______?
B Michael.
A Thank you. [c] ______?
B I'm 32.
A [d] ______?
B No, I'm single.
A OK, thank you. And ...

2 A Well, it's good to see you again, Kerry.
B You too. See you on Saturday?
A Yes, great. [e] ______?
B My mobile number is ... wait a minute ... it's 07445 346799.
A And [f] ______?
B It's kerry.powell@hotweb.co.uk.
A OK, thanks. See you soon.

3 A Right, Dagmara. [g] ______?
B I'm Polish.
A And [h] ______ in London?
B It's 56, New Road, Lewisham.
A [i] ______?
B SW4 6HK.
A Thank you. [j] ______?
B My home number is 020 8533 4689.
A OK. You're in room 6. Your teacher's name is Anna.
B Thank you very much.

b Match pictures A–C to conversations 1–3.

Lost property

Personal possessions

VOCABULARY 1.5

1 Write the vowels (*a*, *e*, *i*, *o*, *u*) in these words.

1 c *o* *a* t
2 w __ ll __ t
3 s __ __ tc __ s __
4 c __ m __ r __
5 __ mbr __ ll __
6 b __ k __
7 sh __ __ s
8 __ D c __ rd
9 l __ pt __ p
10 dr __ ss
11 w __ tch
12 m __ b __ l __

Plurals

VOCABULARY 1.6

2 Write the plurals.

1 a bag
bags
2 a watch
____
3 a man
____
4 a dress
____
5 a person
____
6 a diary
____
7 a hotel
____
8 a woman
____
9 an email address
____
10 a child
____

this, that, these, those

VOCABULARY 1.7

3 Fill in the gaps with *this*, *that*, *these* or *those*.

Reading

4 Read this information. Tick the true sentences. Correct the false sentences.

Learn Fast! Language School Class Register

Level Elementary **Room** 12 **Teacher** Anna Simmons

Name	**Nationality**	**Address in the UK**	**Phone number**
Dagmara Marosz	Polish	56 New Rd SW4 6HK	020 8533 4689 (home)
Evrim Ali	Turkish	3a Grove St E11 4WA	07974 344598 (mobile)
Nina Petrov	Russian	78 West Rd NW1 4TJ	07734 384587 (mobile)
Marcelo Santos	Brazilian	22 High St NW12 3WS	020 8866 8977 (home)

1 Nina is from ~~Germany~~. *Russia*
2 Marcelo is from Brazil. ✓
3 Dagmara's home number is 020 8533 4689.
4 Nina's postcode is NW1 4TJ.
5 Evrim is from Russia.
6 Marcelo's address is 56, New Rd, SW4 6HK.
7 Evrim's home number is 07974 344598.
8 The teacher's surname is Simmons.
9 The class is in room 21.

Reading and Writing Portfolio 1 p64

What's important?

Language Summary 2, Student's Book p130

Adjectives (1) VOCABULARY 2.1

1 **a** Write the vowels (*a*, *e*, *i*, *o*, *u*) in these adjectives.

1 l *a* t *e*
2 s m _ l l
3 y _ _ n g
4 _ x p _ n s _ v _
5 f _ s t
6 b _ _ _ t _ f _ l
7 d _ f f _ c _ l t
8 w r _ n g
9 g _ _ d
10 n _ w

b Write the opposites of the adjectives in **1a**.

1 e*arly*
2 b______
3 o______
4 c______
5 s______
6 u______
7 e______
8 r______
9 b______
10 o______

c Find all the adjectives in **1a** and **1b** (→↓).

B	E	A	U	T	I	F	U	L
I	X	M	C	H	E	A	P	A
G	P	E	A	S	Y	S	T	T
G	E	R	I	G	H	T	L	E
O	N	S	Q	W	R	O	N	G
O	S	M	A	L	L	O	T	R
D	I	F	F	I	C	U	L	T
J	V	Y	Y	O	U	N	G	S
N	E	W	Q	L	F	B	O	L
U	G	L	Y	D	J	A	Y	O
Q	E	A	R	L	Y	D	R	W

Adjective word order and *very* VOCABULARY 2.2

2 Tick the correct sentences. Change the incorrect sentences.

1 This is a very nice bag. ✓
2 Jo's got two ~~beautifuls~~ *beautiful* children. ✗
3 I've got a mobile new.
4 Brad Pitt is my favourite actor.
5 These are expensives shoes.
6 Steve's got a car very old.
7 Mr Lee is a very important man.
8 They've got three bigs dogs.

have got: positive and negative GRAMMAR 2.1

3 Look at the table. Then fill in the gaps with *'s got*, *hasn't got*, *'ve got*, *have got* or *haven't got*.

	 Linda	 Carl	 Jack and Lucy
	✓	✗	✓
	✓	✓	✓
	✗	✗	✓
	✗	✓	✗
	✓	✓	✗

1 Linda *'s got* a laptop.
2 She ______ a camera.
3 She ______ a DVD player.
4 Carl ______ a mobile.
5 He ______ an MP3 player.
6 He ______ a camera.
7 Jack and Lucy ______ a laptop.
8 They ______ an MP3 player.
9 They ______ a DVD player.

have got: questions and short answers GRAMMAR 2.2

4 Make questions with these words.

1 an MP3 player / Linda / Has / got ?
Has Linda got an MP3 player?

2 Has / a laptop / got / Carl ?
____

3 a camera / got / Have / Jack and Lucy ?
____

4 Linda / a mobile / got / Has ?
____

5 a DVD player / got / Has / Carl ?
____

6 a mobile / Jack and Lucy / Have / got ?
____

5 Look again at the table in **3**. Then write short answers to the questions in **4**.

1 *No, she hasn't.*

2 ______________

3 ______________

4 ______________

5 ______________

6 ______________

2B The Browns

Family VOCABULARY 2.3

1 Read about Terry's family. Then write the names on his family tree.

Hi, my name's Terry. I'm married and my wife's name is Megan. We've got one son. His name is George and he's three years old. I've got one sister, Brenda. She's married and her husband's name is Nate. They've got two children. Their daughter's name is Tracy and she's got a brother called David. And my parents? Well, my father's name is Arthur and my mother's name is Shirley. We're a very happy family, I think.

2 Fill in the gaps with these words.

~~grandfather~~	grandchildren	
grandparents	grandmother	
granddaughter	grandsons	
aunt	uncle	cousins

1 Arthur is Tracy and David's *grandfather* .

2 Shirley is their ______________ .

3 Terry is their ______________ .

4 Megan is their ______________ .

5 Tracy, David and George are Arthur and Shirley's ______________ .

6 Tracy is their ______________ .

7 David and George are their ______________ .

8 Tracy and David are George's ______________ .

9 Arthur and Shirley are his ______________ .

Possessive 's GRAMMAR 2.3

3 Look at the picture of Terry's family. Fill in the gaps with the correct names and *'s*.

1 Brenda is *George's* aunt.
2 Terry is ______ brother.
3 Arthur is ______ husband.
4 Nate is ______ uncle.
5 George is Megan and ______ son.
6 Brenda is Tracy and ______ mother.
7 Arthur is Terry and ______ father.
8 Tracy and David are Brenda and ______ children.

4 **a** Write *'s* in the correct place in the sentences.

1 Shirley*'s* got two children, Terry and Brenda.
2 Terry unemployed at the moment.
3 Megan is Terry wife.
4 She got a new laptop.
5 Nate is Brenda husband.
6 He a doctor.

b Does the *'s* in the sentences in **4a** mean *is*, *has* or the possessive?

1 's = *has*
2 's = ______
3 's = ______
4 's = ______
5 's = ______
6 's = ______

Review: question forms

5 **a** Make questions with these words.

1 David's / is / Who / aunt ?
Who is David's aunt?
2 and sisters / got / has / brothers / How many / Terry ?
3 Tracy / grandfather / is / and David's / Who ?
4 children / got / How many / Brenda / has ?
5 parents / and Brenda's / Who / Terry / are ?
6 have / and Shirley / grandchildren / How many / got / Arthur ?
7 is / David / Who / uncle / and Tracy's ?
8 have / Terry / children / How many / and Megan / got ?

b Answer the questions in **5a**.

1 *Megan.*
2 ______
3 ______
4 ______
5 ______
6 ______
7 ______
8 ______

2C REAL WORLD Time and money

Time words VOCABULARY 2.4

1 Fill in the gaps with these words.

~~year~~ day weeks hours days months seconds minutes

1 One *year* = 12 ______ = 52 ______ = 365 ______.

2 One ______ = 24 ______ = 1,440 ______ = 86,400 ______.

Telling the time REAL WORLD 2.1

2 Write these times in two ways.

1 *twenty to eight* *seven forty*

2 ______

3 ______

4 ______

5 ______

6 ______

Talking about the time REAL WORLD 2.2

3 Choose the correct words.

a A What time [1](*is*)/*are* it?
B It's five [2]*past/from* nine.

b A What [3]*hour/time* is your Spanish class?
B It's [4]*at/on* four o'clock.

c A [5]*What/When* time is your brother's English class?
B It's [6]*from/to* six thirty [7]*from/to* eight o'clock.

d A Excuse me. [8]*Have/Are* you got [9]*a/the* time, please?
B Yes, [10]*it/it's* twenty to eleven.
A [11]*Thank/Thanks* very much.
B You're [12]*OK/welcome*.

Buying tickets at the cinema REAL WORLD 2.4

4 Alexis wants to buy tickets at the cinema. Fill in the gaps in the conversation with these sentences.

~~Excuse me~~ Here you are. Right. Thanks a lot. Yes, please. How much is that? Thanks. Bye. What time is the film? Can I have two tickets

ALEXIS [1] *Excuse me*.
TICKET SELLER Yes, can I help you?
ALEXIS [2] ______ for *60 Seconds*, please?
TICKET SELLER Two adults?
ALEXIS [3] ______
TICKET SELLER That's £19.80, please.
ALEXIS [4] ______
TICKET SELLER Thanks. And here are your tickets.
ALEXIS [5] ______
TICKET SELLER Eight forty-five.
ALEXIS [6] ______
TICKET SELLER You're welcome. Enjoy the film.
ALEXIS [7] ______
TICKET SELLER Goodbye.

Where's the baby?

Things in a house VOCABULARY 2.5

1 Look at the picture. Write the words for the things 1–12.

1	*a door*	7	
2		8	
3		9	
4		10	
5		11	
6		12	

Prepositions of place VOCABULARY 2.6

2 Look at the picture in 1 again. Answer these questions. Use these prepositions and the words in brackets.

~~by~~ in on under behind in front of

1 Where's the plant? (desk)
It's by the desk.

2 Where's the bookcase? (sofa)

3 Where's the cat? (coffee table)

4 Where are the mobile phones? (coffee table)

5 Where's the suitcase? (TV)

6 Where are the shoes? (suitcase)

Reading

3 Read Barry's email. Then answer these questions.

To: jackandnancy@onlinemail.org

Hi Jack and Nancy
How are you? Liz and I are on holiday in Canada! We're in a small house in the woods (see photo!) about 20 km from town. It's my cousin Karl's house, but he's in Toronto with his wife and their three children, so only Liz and I are here at the moment. The house isn't very big – it's only got three rooms – but it's very nice. It's beautiful here and it's very quiet. We haven't got a TV or a DVD player, but we've got a lot of books! And we haven't got a computer, but we can send emails from our mobile. Where are you? Are you at home? Please send us an email!
Lots of love Barry

1 Where are Barry and Liz on holiday? *In Canada.*
2 Are they in Barry's cousin's house?
3 How many children has Karl got?
4 How many people are in the cabin?
5 Is the cabin very big?
6 Have they got a TV or a DVD player?
7 Have they got a lot of books?
8 Have they got a computer?

Review: spelling

4 Choose the correct words.

1 miror/mirror (circled: mirror)
2 beautiful/beautifull
3 dificult/difficult
4 smal/small
5 manager/mannager
6 waitres/waitress
7 camera/cammera
8 walet/wallet
9 umbrela/umbrella
10 adress/address

Reading and Writing Portfolio 2 p66

Daily routines VOCABULARY 3.1

1 Which words/phrases do not go with the verbs?

1 **leave** *home/work/~~breakfast~~*
2 **start** *classes/live/work*
3 **have** *breakfast/to bed/lunch/dinner*
4 **go** *lunch/to bed/home*
5 **finish** *work/home/classes*
6 **get** *up/home/bed*

Present Simple (1): positive (*I/you/we/they*) GRAMMAR 3.1

2 Write Barry's sentences about his daily routine. Use the phrases from 1.

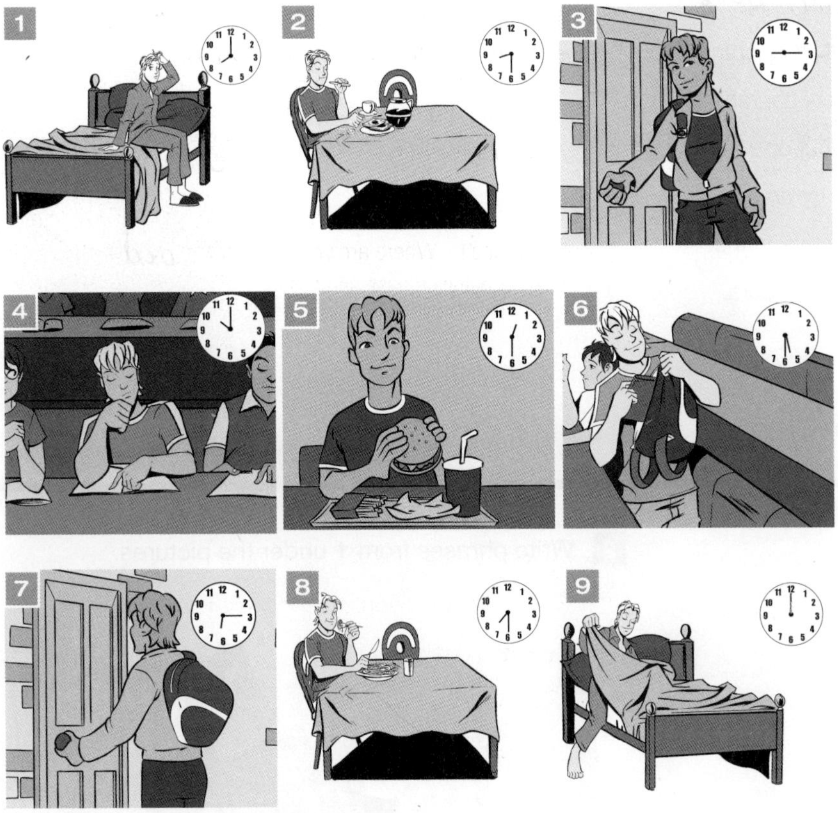

1 I *get up at eight o'clock.*
2 I ______ at ______
3 I ______
4 I ______ classes ______
5 I ______ in the university café.
6 I ______ classes ______
7 I ______
8 I ______
9 I ______

Review: prepositions

3 Fill in the gaps with these prepositions. You can use each preposition more than once.

in	at	for	to	from

1 They have dinner *in* a restaurant.
2 We study ______ the afternoon.
3 I finish work ______ 6.30.
4 Where are you ______ ?
5 I'm ______ Turkey.
6 We have an hour ______ lunch.
7 I live ______ London.
8 They work ______ the morning.
9 I work ______ night.
10 I start work ______ midnight.
11 We study ______ 6 hours a day.
12 My English class is ______ 10.30 ______ 12.30.

Review: subject pronouns and possessive adjectives

4 Choose the correct words.

1 *(I)/My* live in Moscow.
2 Bob's *I/my* brother.
3 Where do *they/their* work?
4 That's *they/their* new car.
5 Is that *she/her* car?
6 Is *she/her* an accountant?
7 Where are *you/your* from?
8 Are *you/your* parents from Russia?
9 Is *he/his* a sales assistant?
10 Is *he/his* brother a doctor?
11 This is *we/our* new DVD player.
12 *We/Our* have a new dog.

Present Simple (1): *Wh-* questions (*I/you/we/they*) GRAMMAR 3.2

5 Read about Hannah and Roy's daily routine. Fill in the gaps with these words/phrases.

~~live~~	have lunch	start work	get up
get home	go to bed	finish work	
have breakfast	sleep	have dinner	

We're theatre actors and we [1] *live* in New York. We [2] ________ at ten o'clock and [3] ________ at home. After breakfast we phone our friends and then we [4] ________ at about three o'clock in a café. We leave home at four o'clock and we [5] ________ at seven in the evening. We [6] ________ at about eleven o'clock and we [7] ________ in a restaurant near the theatre. We [8] ________ at about one o'clock in the morning and then we watch TV for an hour. We [9] ________ at about three o'clock in the morning and [10] ________ for about seven hours.

6 Read about Hannah and Roy again. Write questions with *they* for these answers.

1 Where *do they live?*
They live in New York.

2 What time ________
At ten o'clock.

3 ________
In a café.

4 ________
At four o'clock.

5 ________
In a restaurant near the theatre.

6 ________
At about one o'clock in the morning.

7 ________ after they get home?
They watch TV.

8 ________
At about three o'clock in the morning.

3B Free time

Free time activities (1) VOCABULARY 3.2

1 Fill in the gaps with these words.

~~for~~	to	watch	stay	sport
go	friends	out (x2)	with	

1 go *for* a drink
2 go ________
3 have coffee ________ friends
4 ________ TV
5 go ________ concerts
6 eat ________
7 ________ in
8 ________ shopping
9 do ________
10 phone ________

2 Write phrases from **1** under the pictures.

a *do sport*

b ________

c ________

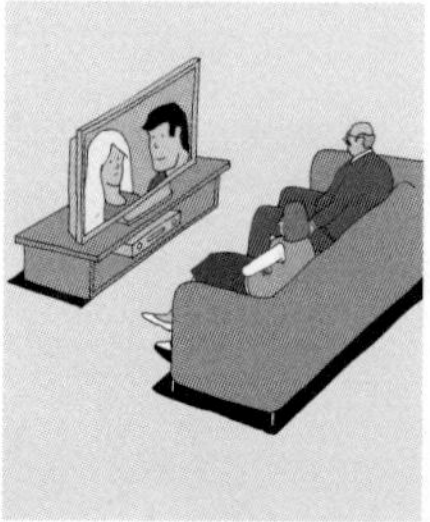

d ________

e ________

f ________

Time phrases with *on*, *in*, *at*, *every* VOCABULARY 3.3

3 Read Glen's email. Choose the correct words.

To: billandjanetclarke@tmail.com

Dear Mum and Dad

Life here in Australia is great! Jessica and I are very happy here and I've got a new job in a computer company! We get up [1] *at/in* seven o'clock [2] *on/every* day and we get home [3] *on/at* about eight [4] *in/every* the evening! We don't go out [5] *in/on* the week, but I go for a drink with friends after work [6] *every/in* Friday and we go to the cinema [7] *on/at* Saturday evening. We don't work [8] *in/at* the weekend, so we get up [9] *at/on* about midday! [10] *On/In* Saturday we go shopping or visit friends [11] *in/at* the afternoon. [12] *At/Every* Sunday we go to Jessica's parents for a barbecue and we leave their house [13] *on/at* about half past eleven [14] *at/in* night!

Lots of love Glen

Present Simple (2): negative (*I/you/we/they*)

GRAMMAR 3.3

4 Read Glen's email again. Tick the true sentences. Make the other sentences negative.

1 Glen and Jessica are very happy in Australia. ✓

2 They get up at six every day.

They don't get up at six every day.

3 They get home at seven in the evening.

______

4 They go out a lot in the week.

______

5 They go to the cinema on Saturday evening.

______

6 They get up early at the weekend.

______

7 Jessica's parents have a barbecue every weekend.

______

Present Simple (2): *yes/no* questions and short answers (*I/you/we/they*) GRAMMAR 3.4

5 Make questions with these words. Then write the short answers.

1 you / in / Do / England / live ?

Do you live in England?

✗ *No, I don't.*

2 your / Do / work / parents ?

______

✗ ______

3 on / go shopping / you / Do / Saturdays ?

______

✓ ______

4 at five / Do / finish / we / o'clock / work ?

______

✗ ______

5 they / go to / Do / a lot / the cinema ?

______

✓ ______

6 at / you / go to / Do / concerts / the weekend ?

______

✓ ______

Review: short answers

6 **a** Match the questions to the short answers.

1 Have they got a car?
2 Is she married?
3 Has he got a laptop?
4 Do you eat out a lot?
5 Are they from France?
6 Do we write the answers?
7 Are you a doctor?
8 Do your sisters work?

a Yes, I am.
b Yes, they do.
c Yes, we do.
d Yes, I do.
e Yes, he has.
f Yes, they have.
g Yes, she is.
h Yes, they are.

b Write negative short answers for the questions in **6a**.

1 *No, they haven't.*
2 ______
3 ______
4 ______
5 ______
6 ______
7 ______
8 ______

3C REAL WORLD Special days

Months VOCABULARY 3.4

1 Write the months. Then put them in the correct order.

a	yuJaarn	1	*January*
b	stuguA		
c	veermNob		
d	liArp		
e	erbtpSmee		
f	yaM		
g	Furryabe		
h	trebOco		
i	unJe		
j	carhM		
k	mceebDre		
l	luJy		

Dates VOCABULARY 3.5

Talking about days and dates REAL WORLD 3.2

2 **a** Write the dates.

1 17/10/09 *17th October 2009*

2 1/1/87 ____________

3 14/5/71 ____________

4 23/7/12 ____________

5 2/2/05 ____________

b Make questions with these words. Then answer the questions.

1 A What / today / date / the / 's ?

What's the date today?

B It's ____________

2 A the / 's / tomorrow / What / date ?

____

B It's ____________

3 A birthday / When / your / 's ?

____

B It's on ____________

4 A mother's / your / 's / When / birthday ?

____

B It's on ____________

Phrases for special days REAL WORLD 3.1

3 Write these phrases for special days.

1 H _ _ _ y b _ _ _ _ h _ _ y!

2 _ a _ p _ N _ _ Y _ _ _ _ !

3 H _ _ p _ a _ _ _ _ v _ _ _ _ _ _ y!

4 C _ _ _ r _ _ _ l _ _ i _ _ s!

Suggestions REAL WORLD 3.3

4 Fill in the gaps in Brian and Nancy's conversation with these phrases.

~~What's the date~~	Let's	I don't think so
on the twenty-fifth	that's a good idea	Maybe
What shall we	Why don't we	What about

NANCY [1] *What's the date* today, Brian?

BRIAN It's the twenty-second, I think.

NANCY It's Eric's birthday [2] ____________ .

BRIAN Is it? [3] ____________ get him?

NANCY [4] ____________ get him a wallet?

BRIAN No, [5] ____________ . He's got a new wallet.

NANCY OK. [6] ____________ a book?

BRIAN [7] ____________ . But he's got lots of books.

NANCY I know! [8] ____________ get him an MP3 player.

BRIAN Yes, [9] ____________ . He hasn't got an MP3 player. I can get one tomorrow.

Early bird?

Frequency adverbs VOCABULARY 3.6

1 Choose the correct answers.

1 Doctors *always/often/never* work at the weekends.
2 Most people *hardly ever/usually/never* go to bed before 3 a.m. in the week.
3 People *sometimes/often/never* live to be 200 years old.
4 People *often/hardly ever/never* watch TV in the evenings.
5 January *always/often/sometimes* has 31 days.
6 June *usually/hardly ever/never* has 28 days.
7 Months *often/hardly ever/never* have 29 days.

Word order of frequency adverbs VOCABULARY 3.7

2 Put the frequency adverbs in the correct places in these sentences.

1 We *never* have dinner before seven in the evening. (never)
2 We're at home on Sunday evenings. (usually)
3 They go to bed after midnight. (often)
4 I'm tired on Monday mornings. (always)
5 I do sport on Saturdays. (sometimes)
6 I have a party on my birthday. (usually)
7 My children get up early at the weekend. (hardly ever)
8 They're at home on New Year's Eve. (never)

Reading

3 Read about Ray's family. Then answer the questions.

1 What do Ray's parents do?
His father's a doctor and his mother's a manager.
2 How many brothers and sisters has Ray got?
______
3 Where do they live?
______
4 Is Jeanette a student?
______
5 How many people have dinner together on Thanksgiving?
______
6 When is Thanksgiving?
______

My name's Ray and [1]**I** live with my parents in Seattle, in the USA. My dad's a doctor and my mum's a manager of a shop. I sometimes help [2]**her** at the weekends. I've also got a brother, Peter, and a sister, Jeanette. Peter's an actor – we sometimes see [3]**him** on TV – and Jeanette's at university. [4]**They** live in California so we don't see [5]**them** very often, but they always come to visit [6]**us** on Thanksgiving every year.
Thanksgiving is a very important holiday in the USA. [7]**It**'s always on the fourth Thursday in November and people usually go home to be with their families. In our house [8]**we** always have a big traditional meal with turkey, corn, sweet potatoes – and pumpkin pie, of course!

Subject and object pronouns GRAMMAR 3.5

4 Look at the words in bold in the text in **3**. Who or what do they talk about?

1 I *Ray*
2 her ______
3 him ______
4 They ______
5 them ______
6 us ______
7 It ______
8 we ______

Reading and Writing Portfolio 3 p68

4A Away from home

Free time activities (2) VOCABULARY 4.1

1 Look at the words/phrases in bold. Fill in the gaps with these verbs.

~~do~~ watch read listen (x2) go (x5) play (x2) take

Hi, my name's Gary, and I live in Wimbledon, in London. I [1] *do* a lot of sport and I often [2] ______ **swimming** or [3] ______ **running** in the week. I always [4] ______ **to the radio** in the morning before I go to work, and when I get home I usually [5] ______ **video games** or [6] ______ **to music**. On Saturday afternoons I often [7] ______ **sport on TV** and and I sometimes [8] ______ **clubbing** with my girlfriend in the evening. Oh, and on Sunday mornings I [9] ______ **to the gym** or [10] ______ **tennis** and then in the afternoon I usually [11] ______ **cycling**. When I'm on holiday I don't do any sport. I usually get up late and [12] ______ lots of **books** – and I always [13] ______ hundreds of **photos**!

Present Simple (3) positive: spelling rules (*he/she/it*) GRAMMAR 4.2

2 Tick the correct *he/she/it* forms. Change the incorrect forms.

1 he works ✓
2 she ~~dos~~ *does*
3 he listens
4 she watchs
5 he reads
6 it gos
7 he teachs
8 she plays
9 it haves
10 she studys

3 Choose the correct words.

1 My sister *work/works* in Italy.
2 I *go/goes* to the cinema every Wednesday.
3 His brother *live/lives* in London.
4 We usually *eat/eats* out at the weekend.
5 My husband *get/gets* home at six.
6 We always *go/goes* shopping on Saturdays.

Present Simple (3): positive and negative (*he/she/it*) GRAMMAR 4.1

4 **a** Look at the table. Then complete the sentences.

	Silvio	Gabriela
home	Milan, Italy	Bogotá, Colombia
job	waiter	Spanish teacher
languages	a little German	very good English
free time	clubbing	tennis

1 Silvio *lives* in Milan, Italy. (live)
2 He ______ in a restaurant. (work)
3 He ______ a little German. (speak)
4 In his free time he ______ clubbing. (go)
5 Gabriela ______ (live)
6 She ______ (teach)
7 She ______ (speak)
8 In her free time she ______ (play)

b Make these sentences negative.

1 Gabriela speaks French.
Gabriela doesn't speak French.
2 Silvio lives in London.
______
3 Silvio works in a language school.
______
4 Silvio and Gabriela live in Turkey.
______
5 Silvio and Gabriela speak Chinese.
______
6 Gabriela teaches English.
______

Review: Present Simple

5 Fill in the gaps. Put the verbs in the correct form of the Present Simple.

Joanne Carling is a journalist and she [1] *works* (work) for News World, a TV news channel. Joanne [2] ________ (not have) a typical daily routine. She [3] ________ (start) work at midnight and she [4] ________ (finish) at six in the morning!

"I usually [5] ________ (go) to bed at about two in the afternoon," says Joanne, "and I [6] ________ (get up) at nine in the evening. Then I [7] ________ (have) 'breakfast' and I usually [8] ________ (get) to work at about ten o'clock."

She [9] ________ (not have) anything to eat at work, but she always [10] ________ (have) a big meal when she [11] ________ (get) home. The morning is her free time and she usually [12] ________ (watch) DVDs or she [13] ________ (do) some sport.

"I [14] ________ (like) my job very much," says Joanne. "But my friends [15] ________ (not like) it at all because they never [16] ________ (see) me!"

4B First Date!

Things you like and don't like VOCABULARY 4.2

1 Write the words.

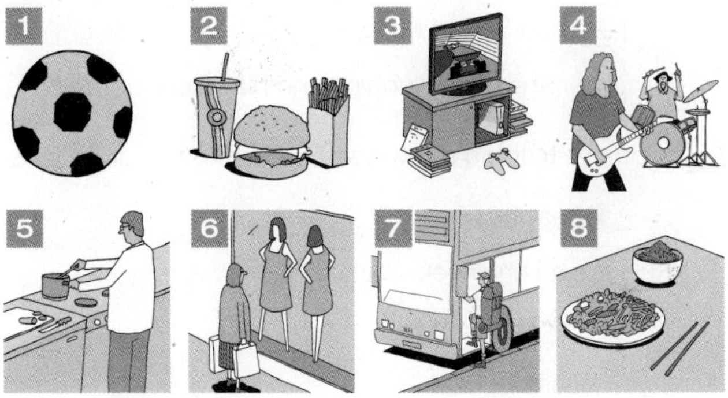

1 f *o o t b a l l*

2 f _ _ _ f _ _ _

3 v _ _ _ _ g _ _ _ _

4 r _ _ _ m _ _ _ _

5 c _ _ _ _ _ _

6 s _ _ _ _ _ _ _ for c _ _ _ _ _ _

7 t _ _ _ _ _ _ _ _

8 C _ _ _ _ _ _ f _ _ _

like/love/hate VOCABULARY 4.3

2 **a** Write these words/phrases in the correct place.

love hate don't quite really OK like

1 I *love* …

2 I ________ like …

3 I ________ …

4 I ________ like …

5 … is ________ .

6 I ________ like …

7 I ________ …

b Look again at the pictures in **2a**. Then complete the sentences about what Josh likes and doesn't like.

1 Josh *really likes* jazz.

2 He ________ dancing.

3 He ________ animals.

4 He thinks reading ________ .

5 He ________ Italian food.

6 He ________ dance music.

7 He ________ cats.

Present Simple (4): questions and short answers (*he/she/it*) GRAMMAR 4.3

3 Read about two more people on the TV game show *First Date!*. Complete the questions and short answers.

Rosie Campbell	
home town	London
job	French teacher
free time	clubbing (on Saturday nights) tennis (on Tuesdays and Thursdays)
likes	dance music, Italian food
doesn't like	cooking, football

First Date!

Hugo Matthews	
home town	Bristol
job	engineer
free time	cycling (at the weekend) watching DVDs (four or five a week)
likes	rock music, Chinese food
doesn't like	video games, fast food

First Date!

ROSIE

1 *Does* Rosie *live* in Manchester? (live)
No, she doesn't.

2 ______ she ______ French? (teach)
______

3 ______ ______ ______ to dance music? (listen)
______

4 ______ ______ ______ cooking? (like)
______

HUGO

5 ______ Hugo ______ in Bristol? (live)
______

6 ______ he ______ in a school? (work)
______

7 ______ ______ ______ fast food? (like)
______

8 ______ ______ ______ a lot of DVDs? (watch)
______

4 **a** Make questions about Rosie with these words.

1 live / Rosie / does / Where ?
Where does Rosie live?

2 she / in her free time / does / do / What ?
______

3 like / What music / does / she ?
______

4 tennis / When / play / she / does ?
______

5 like / does / What food / she ?
______

6 When / clubbing / she / does / go ?
______

b Match answers a–f to questions 1–6 in **4a**.

a [5] Italian food.
b [ ] Dance music.
c [ ] In London.
d [ ] On Tuesdays and Thursdays.
e [ ] On Saturday nights.
f [ ] She goes clubbing and plays tennis.

5 Look at Hugo's answers. Then write the questions.

1 *What does he do?*
He's an engineer.

2 ______
In Bristol.

3 ______
Rock music.

4 ______
Chinese food.

5 ______
He goes cycling and watches DVDs.

6 ______
At the weekend.

Eating out

Food and drink (1) VOCABULARY 4.5

1 Write the words.

1 2 3 4 5 6 7 8

1 a c*heese sandwic*h
2 a b________ and c________
3 a p________
4 a c________ s________
5 a b________ of b________
6 a g________ of r________ w________
7 a b________ of m________ w________
8 a cup of c________

Requests and offers REAL WORLD 4.1

2 **a** Fill in the gaps with these words.

~~order~~	~~you~~	bill	pizzas	I'd	drink	else	What
salad	like	tea	please	Can (x2)	Would (x2)		

1 [W] Would *you* like to *order* now?
2 [ ] Yes, we'd ________ two ________, please.
3 [ ] ________ you like anything ________?
4 [ ] ________ I have a mixed ________, please?
5 [ ] ________ would you like to ________?
6 [ ] ________ like a beer, ________.
7 [ ] ________ you like ________ or coffee?
8 [ ] No, thanks. ________ we have the ________, please?

b Who says sentences 1–8 in **2a**? Write W (waiter) or C (customer).

3 **a** Rob and Sue are in a restaurant. Make sentences with these words.

1 now / you / Would / like / to order ? — WAITER 1 *Would you like to order now?*
2 Yes, / and / the / I'd / chips / like / burger / please . — ROB 2 ________
3 salad, / And / have / please / I / the / tuna / can ? — SUE 3 ________
4 you / to / drink / like / would / What ? — WAITER 4 ________
5 of / like / wine / a bottle / red / We'd . — ROB 5 ________
6 you / dessert / like / a / Would ? — WAITER 6 ________
7 I / apple / can / pie / the / Yes, / have ? — ROB 7 ________
8 I'd / like / the / please / salad, / And / fruit . — SUE 8 ________
9 else / you / anything / Would / like ? — WAITER 9 ________
10 coffees, / Yes, / please / two . — SUE 10 ________
11 we / the / please / And / bill, / can / have ? — ROB 11 ________

b Read the conversation again. What do Rob and Sue order?

Breakfast time

Food and drink (2) VOCABULARY 4.6

1 Do the puzzle. Find the food (↓).

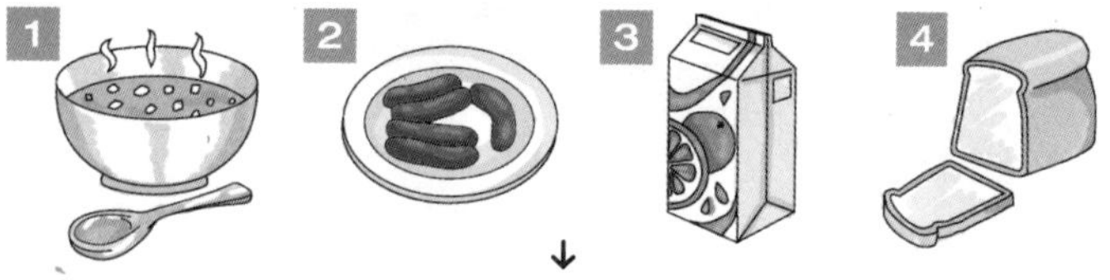

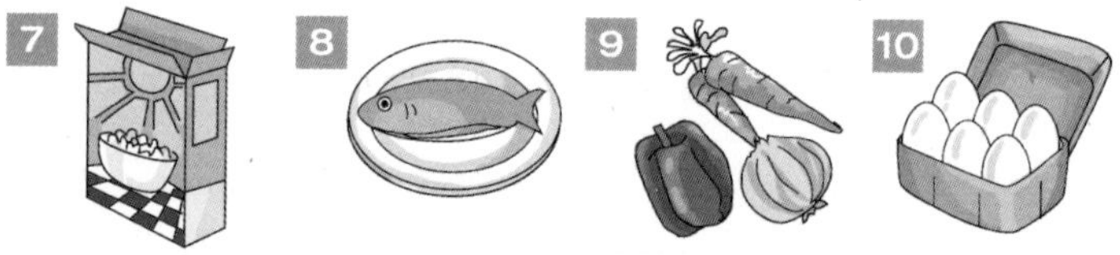

Countable and uncountable nouns

VOCABULARY 4.7

2 Fill in the gaps with *a*, *an* or – .

1 I'd like *a* bottle of *–* beer, please.
2 I love ___ fish, but I never eat ___ meat.
3 I have ___ apple and ___ banana every day.
4 We eat ___ bread every day, but we don't usually eat ___ rice.
5 Dave has ___ tuna sandwich every lunchtime.
6 Do you eat ___ olives or ___ tomatoes?
7 Can I have ___ glass of orange juice, please?
8 He has ___ croissant and ___ milk for breakfast.
9 I often have ___ toast and ___ jam for breakfast.
10 I'd like ___ bottle of ___ water, please.

Reading

3 Read the article. Are these sentences true (T) or false (F)?

1 *T* Chinese people eat a lot of rice.
2 ☐ Tea in Tibet is different to tea in the UK.
3 ☐ You can buy beef in every McDonald's restaurant in the world.
4 ☐ Japanese people eat a lot of chocolate.
5 ☐ The menu at the Royal Dragon restaurant is very big.
6 ☐ It is easy to have dinner at the Solo per Due restaurant.

www.amazingfoodfacts.com

Amazing food facts!

We all love food, but we don't all like the same things. Read these amazing food facts from around the world and see how different we are.

- People in China eat about 135,000,000,000 kgs of rice a year – more than in any other country in the world.
- In Tibet, people don't have sugar in their tea, they have butter – and salt!
- In McDonald's restaurants in India they don't sell beef. All the meat in their burgers is chicken or lamb. They also sell vegetarian burgers.
- People in Ireland drink about 150 litres of beer a year. In Germany, people drink about 130 litres a year.
- American people eat about 10 kg of chocolate every year, but Japanese people eat only 3 kg a year.
- The Royal Dragon restaurant in Bangkok, Thailand, has space for 5,000 customers at one time. There are 1,000 waiters and cooks, and over 1,000 items on the menu. The restaurant also has 24,500 plates!
- The Solo per Due restaurant in Vacone, in central Italy, has only got one table – for two people!

Reading and Writing Portfolio 4 p70

Adjectives (2) VOCABULARY 5.1

1 **a** Write the adjectives. Then write their opposites.

1	het mase	t *he same*	d *ifferent*
2	tique	q	n
3	rongib	b	i
4	liferynd	f	u
5	latl	t	s
6	ypahp	h	u
7	lewl	w	i
8	kycul	l	u
9	toh	h	c
10	icfstnaat	f	a
11	mzaagni	a	t

b Which of these adjectives do <u>not</u> go with the nouns?

1 A *hot/cold/~~friendly~~* day.
2 A *short/cold/wonderful* country.
3 A *happy/hot/lucky* family.
4 A *tall/quiet/friendly* café.
5 An *interesting/ill/amazing* city.
6 A *noisy/quiet/well* place.
7 An *amazing/unhappy/awful* restaurant.
8 A *terrible/short/boring* job.

Past Simple (1): *be* (positive and negative) GRAMMAR 5.1

2 Read about Matt's holiday in the USA in 1994. Choose the correct words.

When I [1](*was*)/*were* thirteen my best friend [2]*was/were* Andy. We [3]*was/were* in the same class at school. Ten years later, in 1994, Andy and I [4]*was/were* on holiday in Miami, in the USA. One evening there [5]*was/were* a party in our hotel. There [6]*wasn't/weren't* any other English people at the party – they [7]*was/were* all American. There [8]*was/were* one very beautiful woman at the party called Penny. She [9]*wasn't/weren't* very friendly at first – but two years later we [10]*was/were* husband and wife! Our son, Jason, [11]*was/were* born four years later in Bristol, where we live now. It [12]*was/were* his thirteenth birthday yesterday!

Past Simple (1): *be* (questions and short answers) GRAMMAR 5.2

3 **a** Make questions with these words.

1 Andy / Was / best friend / Matt's ?
Was Andy Matt's best friend?

2 class / Matt and Andy / the same / Were / in ?

3 the USA / Was / 1992 / in / Matt / in ?

4 the party / Matt and Andy's hotel / Was / at ?

5 at first / Penny / friendly / very / Was ?

6 Matt and Penny / 1994 / married / Were / in ?

7 Bristol / Jason / born / Was / in ?

8 it / yesterday / Was / birthday / Jason's ?

b Write short answers to the questions in **3a**.

1 *Yes, he was.*
2
3
4
5
6
7
8

4 Read about 1994. Then fill in the gaps with these question words and *was* or *were*.

~~Where~~	Who	How old	What	When (x2)

1 _*Where*_ _*was*_ the football World Cup in 1994?
In the USA.

2 ________ ________ the final?
On 17th July.

3 ________ ________ the President of the USA?
Bill Clinton.

4 ________ ________ the South African general election?
In April 1994.

5 ________ ________ the most popular films?
The Lion King and *Forrest Gump*.

6 ________ ________ Tom Hanks in 1994?
He was 38.

1994

- The football World Cup was in the USA. The final was between Italy and Brazil on 17th July, 1994. Brazil won 3–2 on penalties.
- In 1994 Bill Clinton was the President of the USA. John Major was the British Prime Minister and Boris Yeltsin was the Russian President.
- There was a general election in South Africa in April 1994. Nelson Mandela became the first black President of South Africa.
- *The Lion King* and *Forrest Gump* were the most popular films in the USA. Tom Hanks, who won an Oscar for best actor in *Forrest Gump*, was 38 at the time.

5B Famous films

Life events VOCABULARY 5.3

1 Choose the correct verbs.

1 *meet*/*(leave)* school
2 *move/make* a film
3 *meet/win* my husband
4 *get/make* married
5 *meet/write* a book
6 *study/move* English
7 *write/have* children
8 *get/move* house
9 *win/meet* an Oscar
10 *become/win* a film director
11 *win/leave* the lottery
12 *move/study* to England
13 *become/study* physics
14 *get/have* divorced
15 *become/have* famous
16 *have/win* a dream
17 *make/meet* my wife
18 *study/leave* university
19 *make/write* a letter
20 *meet/make* a lot of money

Past Simple (2): regular and irregular verbs (positive) GRAMMAR 5.3

2 **a** Write the Past Simple of these regular verbs.

1 play	*played*	5 study	________	9 marry	________
2 start	________	6 look	________	10 want	________
3 visit	________	7 live	________	11 like	________
4 love	________	8 work	________	12 stop	________

b Fill in the gaps with the Past Simple forms of these irregular verbs.

~~have~~	meet	get	leave	become
make	go	win	write	be

1 My grandparents _*had*_ five boys and two girls.
2 Yolanda and Steve ________ married in July last year.
3 John F Kennedy ________ President of the USA in 1961.
4 I ________ £1,000 on the lottery last weekend!
5 I ________ my husband when I ________ to Turkey in 2002.
6 After Gary ________ school he ________ children's books.
7 My uncle ________ a lot of money when he ________ young.

Review: Past Simple

3 Read about an actor and an actress who appeared in James Cameron's films. Put the verbs in the Past Simple.

Arnold Schwarzenegger

Arnold Schwarzenegger 1 *was* (be) born in Austria on July 30th 1947. He 2 ______ (move) to the USA when he was 21. He 3 ______ (study) business at the University of Wisconsin and he also 4 ______ (want) to be an actor. He 5 ______ (make) the first *Terminator* film, directed by James Cameron, in 1984 and *Terminator 2: Judgement Day* in 1991. He was also in the third *Terminator* film: *Terminator 3: Rise of the Machines* in 2003. Then he 6 ______ (become) a politician and he 7 ______ (be) Governor of California from 2003 to 2011. Arnold 8 ______ (meet) TV journalist Maria Schriver, in 1977 and they 9 ______ (get) married in 1986.

Sigourney Weaver

Susan Weaver 10 ______ (be) born on October 8th 1949 in New York City. She 11 ______ (change) her name to Sigourney Weaver when she 12 ______ (be) a teenager. She 13 ______ (study) English literature at Stanford University and drama in New York. She 14 ______ (become) famous in 1979 when she 15 ______ (win) an Oscar for her performance as Ellen Ripley in *Alien*. She 16 ______ (make) three more *Alien* films – *Aliens*, directed by James Cameron, *Alien 3* and *Alien: Resurrection*. Sigourney 17 ______ (marry) another director, Jim Simpson, in 1984 and they have one child.

Past Simple (2): *Wh-* questions GRAMMAR 5.4

4 Fill in the gaps in these questions. There is one gap for each word.

1 *Where* *was* Arnold Schwarzenegger born?
In Austria.

2 When ______ he ______ to the USA?
When he was 21.

3 ______ ______ he ______ the first *Terminator* film?
In 1984.

4 ______ ______ years ______ he Governor of California?
Eight years.

5 ______ ______ he ______ married to in 1986?
Maria Schriver.

6 ______ ______ Sigourney Weaver ______ ?
On October 8th 1949.

7 ______ ______ she ______ her name?
When she was a teenager.

8 ______ ______ she ______ at Stanford University?
English literature.

9 ______ ______ she ______ an Oscar?
In 1979.

10 ______ ______ *Alien* films ______ she ______ ?
Four.

Review: Past Simple questions

5 **a** Fill in the gaps with *did*, *was* or *were*.

1 Where *were* you born?

2 Where ______ you live when you ______ a child?

3 ______ your parents born in the same country as you?

4 What ______ you do last night?

5 When ______ your last English class?

6 Where ______ you go last weekend?

7 Where ______ your father live when he ______ young?

8 ______ it cold last night?

9 When ______ you start learning English?

10 What ______ you have for breakfast this morning?

b Answer the questions for you.

Four weekends

Weekend activities VOCABULARY 5.4

1 Yvonne lives in Melbourne, Australia. Read her blog. Then fill in the gaps with the Past Simple of the verbs in the boxes.

~~stay~~	be	go to	get	do
go for	clean (x2)	have		

www.yvonnesspace.net

Yvonne's space

Saturday 14th October

I [1] *stayed* in bed until nine thirty and then I [2] ______ the house and [3] ______ the washing. David [4] ______ the car in the morning and we [5] ______ a walk together in the afternoon. David [6] ______ very tired when we [7] ______ home, so he went to bed. In the evening I [8] ______ the cinema with Katy and we [9] ______ a great time. Bed at midnight.

stay	do	go to	go for
watch (x2)	write (x2)	have	

www.yvonnesspace.net

Sunday 15th October

I [10] ______ a run in the morning, but David [11] ______ a bad cold, so he [12] ______ at home and [13] ______ TV. I [14] ______ my parents' house for lunch and then in the afternoon I [15] ______ a long email to our son, Harry – he's in South America at the moment. In the evening I [16] ______ my Spanish homework and [17] ______ a report for work. Then I [18] ______ a DVD with David before bed. Why are there only two days in a weekend?!

Showing interest REAL WORLD 5.1
Asking follow-up questions REAL WORLD 5.2

2 **a** Yvonne is at work on Monday morning. Read the conversation. Then choose the correct responses 1–6.

YVONNE Hi, Stuart. How was your weekend?
STUART It was fantastic! I went away for the weekend.
YVONNE [1]*(Oh, great!)/What a shame.* [a] *Where did you go?*
STUART To Sydney.
YVONNE [2]*Oh dear./Wow!* [b] ______?
STUART It was beautiful. We had a wonderful time.
YVONNE [c] ______?
STUART With Linda, my girlfriend. It was her birthday.
YVONNE [3]*Oh, nice./You're joking!* [d] ______?
STUART We went to the Opera House and did lots of shopping – you know, the usual things.
YVONNE [e] ______?
STUART In a nice little hotel near Bondi Beach.
YVONNE It sounds great!
STUART Yes, it was. So how was your weekend?
YVONNE It was fine, very quiet. My husband, David, was in bed with a cold.
STUART [4]*Oh, great!/Oh, dear.* Is he OK now?
YVONNE No, he isn't.
STUART [5]*What a shame./Wow!* [f] ______?
YVONNE I went to the cinema.
STUART [6]*You're joking!/Oh, right.* [g] ______?
YVONNE It was called 'Frank's Happiness'.
STUART Oh yes, I know it. What did you …

b Make questions with these words and write them in the correct places a–g in **2a**.

1 go / did / you / Where ?
2 did / What / do / there / you ?
3 did / stay / Where / you ?
4 like / it / What / was ?
5 go / Who / with / you / did ?
6 you / evening / do / did / Saturday / on / What ?
7 did / What / see / you ?

Competitions

Adjectives (3) VOCABULARY 5.5

1 Find 12 adjectives (→↓).

S	E	C	R	(E	X	C	I	T	E	D)
B	O	R	E	D	O	R	I	C	H	E
U	C	O	E	M	P	T	Y	P	L	A
S	H	W	Q	F	A	M	T	O	X	P
Y	I	D	A	N	G	E	R	O	U	S
C	L	E	A	N	M	L	E	R	E	A
T	J	D	I	R	T	Y	R	A	U	F
C	O	M	F	O	R	T	A	B	L	E

Adjectives with *very*, *really*, *quite*, *too*

VOCABULARY 5.6

2 **a** Choose the correct words in these conversations.

1

A Wow! That's a ^{1}*(really)/too* big TV.

B Yes, I bought it last week. It was ^{2}*too/very* expensive.

2

A Do you want to come to the Caritas club tonight? It's ^{3}*quite/too* cheap and the music's ^{4}*really/too* good.

B No, I hate that place. It's always ^{5}*too/quite* crowded.

3

A Hi, Chris. You look ^{6}*quite/really* happy today.

B Yes, I won £10 million on the lottery last weekend!

4

A Mum, can we go and see *Dead Again*?

B Sorry, you're ^{7}*very/too* young. It's for people over 18.

b Match conversations 1–4 to pictures A–D.

A

B

C

D

Reading

3 **a** Read the email about Ruth's weekend. Change the incorrect words in bold.

To: ellenroberts99@gomail.net

Hi Ellen

Do you remember that ^{1}~~**me**~~ *my* boyfriend Phil ^{2}~~**win**~~ *won* a competition last June? Well, last weekend we went ^{3}**in** Paris! It ^{4}**were** amazing! We travelled first class on the plane and stayed in a ^{5}**too** beautiful hotel by the River Seine. On Saturday afternoon we ^{6}**walk** around the city and ^{7}**go** to the Louvre Museum. Then in the evening we went to a classical concert – it was ^{8}**too** good. On Sunday we ^{9}**have** breakfast by the river and it ^{10}**were** very romantic. Then ^{11}**on** the afternoon we went up the Eiffel Tower. When we ^{12}**was** at the top Phil asked me to marry ^{13}**he**! I said yes, of course! Then we had dinner in a wonderful restaurant and we ^{14}**arrive** back in London ^{15}**in** about midnight. It was a fantastic weekend!

Speak soon. Ruth

b Read the email again. Then complete sentences 1–8 with when they did these things.

1 Phil and Ruth went to Paris *last weekend* .
2 They went up the Eiffel Tower *on Sunday afternoon* .
3 They went to a museum ______ .
4 They had breakfast by the river ______ .
5 They walked around the city ______ .
6 They went to a classical concert ______ .
7 They arrived back in London ______ .
8 Phil won a competition ______ .

Reading and Writing Portfolio 5 p72

The internet VOCABULARY 6.1

1 Fill in the gaps with the correct form of these verbs.

~~use~~	chat	use	read
get	send	go	have (x2)
download (x2)			

1 I *use* the internet for about six hours every day.

2 Last night I ______ online to buy some concert tickets.

3 I like ______ blogs about other people's holidays.

4 Do you ______ a favourite website?

5 I never buy CDs because I ______ music onto my MP3 player instead.

6 My son ______ to his friends online for about three hours a day.

7 I always ______ the same search engine.

8 I sometimes ______ videos onto my laptop so I can watch them on the train.

9 Excuse me. Does this café ______ WiFi?

10 I ______ you an email yesterday. Did you ______ it?

2 Read about Jeff Bezos and Amazon.com. Put the verbs in the Past Simple.

www.internetbillionaires.com/jeffbezos

The World's Bookshop

amazon.com

Jeff Bezos [1] *was* (be) born in 1964 in New Mexico, USA, and when he [2] ______ (be) a child he [3] ______ (work) on his parents' farm. Jeff [4] ______ (go) to Princeton University and [5] ______ (study) electrical engineering and computer science. After he [6] ______ (leave) university he [7] ______ (work) on Wall Street in New York, but he [8] ______ (want) to start his own internet company.

He [9] ______ (have) the idea for Amazon in the car when he and his wife [10] ______ (be) on a long drive from New York to Seattle in 1994. At first he [11] ______ (call) the company Cadabra, but then he [12] ______ (change) the name to Amazon, after the river in Brazil. Amazon [13] ______ (sell) its first book in July 1995, and by September it [14] ______ (have) sales of $20,000 a week. At first Amazon only [15] ______ (sell) books, then in 1998 it [16] ______ (start) selling CDs. Now you can buy almost anything on Amazon – DVDs, video games, computers, software, TVs, clothes and things for the house. The company sells over $10 billion of products a year, and he is now a billionaire.

Past Simple (3): negative GRAMMAR 6.1

3 Tick the true sentences. Make the other sentences negative.

1 Jeff Bezos was born in New Mexico, USA. ✓

2 He went to Stanford University. *He didn't go to Stanford University.*

3 He studied electrical engineering and computer science.

______

4 He worked in Los Angeles.

______

5 He had the idea for Amazon on a plane.

______

6 Amazon was the first name for the website.

______

7 Amazon sold its first book in July 1995.

______

8 The website started selling CDs in 1996.

______

Past Simple (3): *yes/no* questions and short answers

GRAMMAR 6.2

4 Make questions with these words.

1 Born / Jeff Bezos / Was / 1966 / in ?

Was Jeff Bezos born in 1966?

2 Jeff Bezos / Did / Princeton University / go to ?

____

3 study / he / Did / university / at / physics ?

____

4 the idea / Did / in the car / have / he / for Amazon ?

____

5 the first name / Cadabra / for the website / Was ?

____

6 its first book / sell / June 1995 / Amazon / in / Did ?

____

7 start / 1998 / in / Amazon / selling / Did / CDs ?

____

5 Read the article about Jeff Bezos again. Then write the short answers to the questions in **4**.

1 *No, he wasn't.*
2 ________
3 ________
4 ________
5 ________
6 ________
7 ________

Review: Past Simple

6 Correct these sentences.

1 I ~~go~~ *went* to the cinema last night.
2 Where was you born?
3 What time did you started work?
4 He stop work at ten last night.
5 Where they were last night?
6 I didn't watched TV yesterday.
7 When was he born?
8 I not play tennis last weekend.

6B Changing technology

Mobile phones and TVs

VOCABULARY 6.2

1 Fill in the gaps with these words.

~~send~~ get GPS channel TV programme apps battery charge record turn on turn off

1 I usually *send* about thirty texts a day.
2 What time is your favourite ________ on?
3 Can you ________ the TV? There's a good film on at 9.00.
4 Don't forget to ________ the TV before you go to bed.
5 I need to buy a new ________ for my mobile.
6 Did you ________ the text I sent you yesterday?
7 Which ________ is *The Simpsons* on?
8 I've got about fifty ________ on my mobile.
9 I sometimes ________ films so I can watch them again.
10 Excuse me. Where can I ________ my phone?
11 I've got ________ on my mobile. I often use it when I'm in the car.

Past time phrases

VOCABULARY 6.3

2 **a** Fill in the gaps with *ago*, *last* or *in*.

1 I was born *in* 1994.
2 I went on holiday ________ year.
3 I went to a party three weeks ________ .
4 My birthday is ________ January.
5 I watched a lot of TV ________ night.
6 I left school ________ 2008.
7 I had breakfast six hours ________ .
8 I went to the cinema ________ week.
9 My parents were born ________ the seventies.
10 I did some sport ________ weekend.
11 I went shopping two days ________ .
12 I bought my mobile two years ________ .

b Tick the sentences in **2a** that are true for you.

can/can't; could/couldn't GRAMMAR 6.3

3 Choose the correct words in these sentences.

1 In the fifties you *can't/couldn't* watch TV in colour.

2 You *can/could* watch TV in colour in the seventies, but in the UK you *couldn't/could* only get three channels. Now people *can/could* get hundreds of different channels on their TVs.

3 I got my first mobile phone in 1995. It *can/could* send and receive texts, but it *could/couldn't* take photos or go online. With my new phone I *can/could* download TV programmes and make videos.

4 You *can't/couldn't* buy a 3D TV in the nineties. Now you *can/could* buy 3D TVs for your home and you *can/could* see a lot of 3D films at the cinema.

5 I love this café – you *can/couldn't* get food from all over the world here. It's also got free WiFi, so you *can/can't* use the internet here too. The problem is, it's always very crowded so you *can/can't* find a seat!

4 Correct the mistakes in these sentences.

1 ~~Do you can~~ *Can you* make video calls on your phone?

2 Could you records programmes in 1974?

3 Can I charging my phone here, please?

4 Can you download videos into your laptop?

5 I can to watch TV on my mobile.

6 I met him about ago six years.

7 My parents went to Spain on 2010.

8 I didn't got a text from you yesterday.

9 Did your sister called you last night?

10 I often chat at my friends online.

11 I was borned in Buenos Aires.

12 We went to the cinema weekend last.

5 Silvio and Francesca are on holiday in the UK. Read signs 1–8. Then write short answers to these questions.

1 a Can Silvio and Francesca park here? *Yes, they can.*
b Can they stay for six hours? ____________

2 Silvio wants to have a cigarette. Can he smoke here? ____________

3 Can Francesca use her mobile here? ____________

4 Silvio and Francesca have got two children aged 18 and 19. Can they come in here? ____________

5 a Silvio's got a car. It's 11 a.m. on Sunday. Can he drive here? ____________
b It's 6.30 p.m. on Friday. Can he drive here? ____________

6 a It's 3 p.m. on Sunday. Can Silvio park here? ____________
b It's 9 a.m. on Tuesday. Can he park here? ____________

7 Can Silvio and Francesca's children take their dog in here? ____________

8 Can Silvio and Francesca go in here? ____________

The news

Verbs from news stories VOCABULARY 6.4

1 Write the Past Simple of these verbs. Which are regular (R)? Which are irregular (I)?

1 damage *damaged R*
2 buy ______
3 crash ______
4 say ______
5 tell ______
6 save ______
7 receive ______
8 find ______
9 lose ______
10 sail ______
11 put ______
12 die ______

Reading

2 **a** Read the news reports. Then match headlines A–C to news reports 1–3.

A ☐ EARTHQUAKE KILLS FOUR IN LOS ANGELES

B ☐ 24-HOUR CINEMA OPENS IN LONDON

C ☐ TEACHER LOSES WINNING TICKET

1 Last Saturday Mark Watt, a 48-year-old teacher from Maidstone, thought he was a very rich man. He had all seven correct numbers on the EuroMillions lottery and went clubbing to celebrate with his friends. The next day he looked in his wallet for the ticket – but it wasn't there! "Maybe I lost it," said Mark. "Or maybe one of my friends stole it."

2 At least four people died in this morning's earthquake in Los Angeles, California. The earthquake started at 7.38 a.m. when many people were on their way to work. About a thousand people are still without water or electricity and there are no buses or trains in the city today.

3 The UK's first 24-hour cinema opened last night in the centre of London. The new cinema, called Twentyfourseven, is open 24 hours a day and has 15 screens. The manager of the cinema, Jamie Harris, said, "Our first night was very successful. We had two hundred people for the film that started at 3.15 in the morning and they all had a great time."

b Read the news reports again. Answer these questions.

1 Why was Mark Watt happy last Saturday?
Because he thought he was very rich.
2 Where did he put the lottery ticket?
______
3 What time did the earthquake start?
______
4 How many people don't have water or electricity?
______
5 What's the name of the new cinema?
______
6 How many people were at the 3.15 a.m. film last night?
______

Talking about the news REAL WORLD 6.1

3 Read these conversations. Fill in the gaps with the phrases in the boxes.

~~Did you hear about~~	Really?	No, where was it?
Oh no, that's terrible.	Oh, that's good.	Is she OK?

A [1] *Did you hear about* that earthquake?
B [2] ______
A In California. At least four people died.
B [3] ______
A Yes, and my sister lives in Los Angeles.
B [4] ______ [5] ______
A Yes, she's fine. So are her family.
B [6] ______

You're joking!	No, what happened?
Did you read about	

A [7] ______ the man who won the lottery?
B [8] ______
A He lost the ticket!
B [9] ______
A Yes, he thinks maybe one of his friends took it!

Mario man

Articles: *a*, *an* and *the* VOCABULARY 6.5

1 Read the joke and fill in the gaps with *a* or *the*.

One day [1] _a_ horse walked into [2] ______ bar and ordered [3] ______ drink. "Can I have [4] ______ bottle of beer, please?" said [5] ______ horse. "Er ... sure," said [6] ______ barman. He gave a bottle of beer to [7] ______ horse. [8] ______ horse drank [9] ______ beer and gave [10] ______ bottle back to [11] ______ barman. "How much is that?" he asked. "That's, er, twenty pounds," said [12] ______ barman. [13] ______ horse gave him [14] ______ twenty-pound note. "We don't get many talking horses in here," said the barman. "I'm not surprised if beer is twenty pounds a bottle," said the horse.

Reading

2 **a** Read the questionnaire. Choose the correct words.

Top tips for learning English

Do you ...

1 ... study English at (a)/*the* language school?
2 ... watch or listen to *a/the* news online in English?
3 ... work for *a/the* British or American company?
4 ... go and see films in English at *a/the* cinema?
5 ... have *an/the* English dictionary?
6 ... practise English *a/the* lot outside class?
7 ... have *an/the* English grammar book?
8 ... always look at *a/the* Language Summaries in *a/the* back of *a/the* Student's Book?
9 ... use *a/the* face2face DVD-ROM?
10 ... think English is *a/the* really interesting language to learn?

b Answer the questions for you. How many *yes* answers have you got? Check your score in the Answer Key.

Review: prepositions

3 Fill in the gaps with these prepositions. You can use each preposition more than once.

at	from	with	for	to	in	on

1 I don't work _at_ the weekend.
2 I get up ______ nine o'clock.
3 She slept ______ eight hours.
4 We're ______ Japan. We're Japanese.
5 It's my birthday ______ Monday.
6 Would you like to go ______ a drink?
7 I often work ______ night.
8 I often have coffee ______ friends.
9 My son was born ______ 2002.
10 Do you often go ______ the theatre?
11 I sometimes sleep ______ the afternoon.
12 I never watch sport ______ TV.
13 Do you often listen ______ the radio?
14 The party is ______ March 22nd.
15 Do you live ______ a big city?
16 I went ______ a run last night.

Review: spelling

4 Circle the words with the correct spelling.

1 Munday/(Monday)
2 favourite/favourate
3 January/Janaury
4 eighteen/eihgteen
5 diferent/different
6 frendly/friendly
7 dangerus/dangerous
8 bisciuts/biscuits
9 duaghter/daughter
10 crowded/crowdid
11 swimming/swiming
12 divorsed/divorced
13 vegetables/vegtables
14 granfather/grandfather
15 shoping/shopping
16 Wensday/Wednesday
17 chocolate/choclate
18 intresting/interesting
19 burthday/birthday
20 tomatos/tomatoes

Reading and Writing Portfolio 6 p74

Places in a town

VOCABULARY 7.1

1 Look at the map of Tayford, a small town in England. Then match these words to places 1–12.

a pub [8]	a hotel [ ]
a station [ ]	houses [ ]
flats [ ]	a road [ ]
a market [ ]	a square [ ]
a café [ ]	shops [ ]
a bus station [ ]	a park [ ]

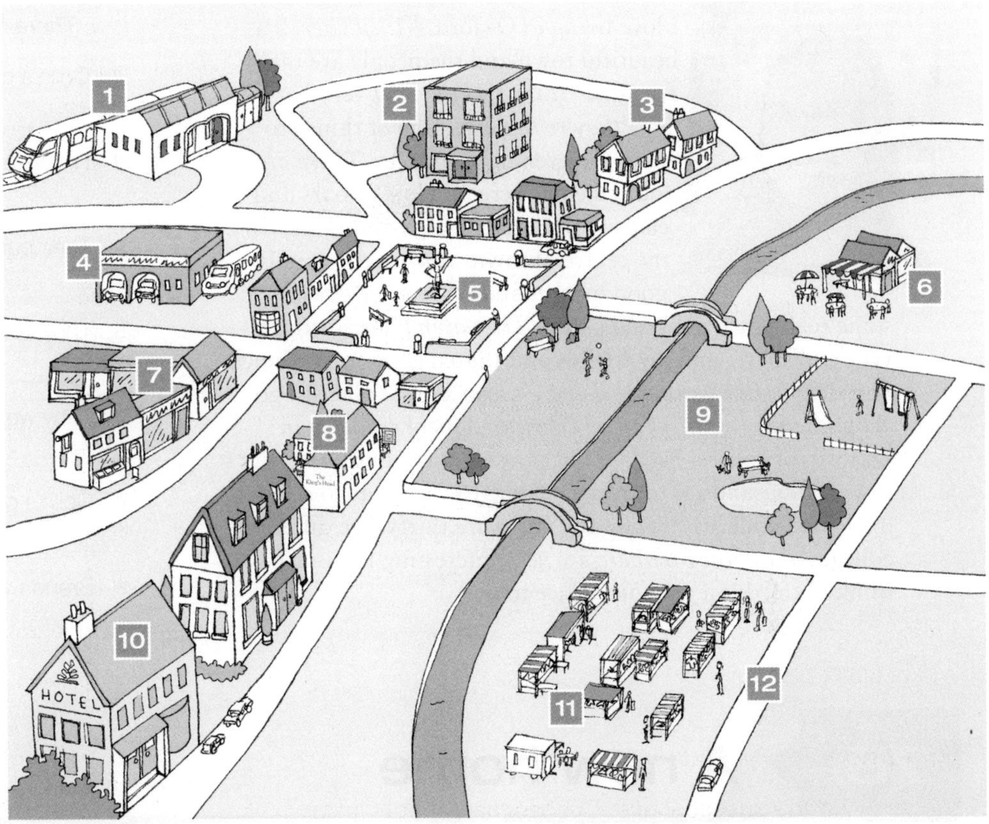

there is/there are

GRAMMAR 7.1

2 Read what Colin says about Tayford. Fill in the gaps with *there's*, *there are*, *there isn't* or *there aren't*.

Tayford is a really great place to live and lots of tourists visit the town in the summer. 1 *There are* lots of shops and 2 __________ a nice park in the centre. 3 __________ two or three really nice hotels and some very nice pubs and bars. 4 __________ also four or five very good restaurants. On Saturdays and Sundays 5 __________ an interesting market, but 6 __________ a market every day, only at the weekend. 7 __________ a lot of beautiful buildings in Tayford – some of them are over 500 years old – but 8 __________ any museums. 9 __________ also a small theatre, but 10 __________ a cinema. 11 __________ a station with trains every hour to Oxford and to London. 12 __________ also a bus station in Tayford, but 13 __________ an airport near the town.

3 Complete the questions about Tayford. Then write the short answers.

1 *Is there* a station?
Yes, there is.

2 __________ any museums?
____

3 __________ a park?
____

4 __________ any flats?
____

5 __________ a cinema?
____

6 __________ any restaurants?
____

7 __________ an airport?
____

8 __________ bus station?
____

Review: *there, they* and *it*

4 Colin's sister, Brenda, lives in Oxford. Read about the town. Then choose the correct answers.

I love living in Oxford. 1 *(It's)/There's* a beautiful town and the people are really friendly. 2 *It isn't/There isn't* very big but 3 *they're/there* are lots of things to do in the evening. 4 *They are/There are* four cinemas here and lots of bars and clubs with different food and music. In the centre of town 5 *it's/there's* a really good market and 6 *they are/there are* some really nice pubs and cafés. 7 *They aren't/There aren't* very expensive, and my friends and I often go there for lunch or a drink after work. 8 *It's/There's* also a great place to go shopping for food. 9 *They're/There are* lots of students in Oxford, of course, because 10 *it's/there's* a famous university town. Thousands of tourists come here every year to see the university colleges. 11 *They are/There are* thirty-five different colleges and 12 *they're/there are* very interesting to visit. I think Oxford is a very nice place to live.

Review: negative verb forms

5 Make these sentences negative.

1 There's an airport.
There isn't an airport.

2 Colin's got a new car.
....

3 His sister works in Tayford.
....

4 Their parents live in London.
....

5 They've got a big house.
....

6 They went to Oxford last year.
....

7 Colin's grandparents were doctors.
....

8 Brenda was born in Tayford.
....

7B A new home

Rooms and things in a house VOCABULARY 7.2

1 Do the puzzle. Find the thing in a house (↓).

How much ... ? and *How many ... ?* GRAMMAR 7.2

2 Read the quiz. Fill in the gaps with *How much* or *How many*. Then choose the correct answers.

How much do you know?

1 *How many* states are there in the USA?
There are *49/(50)/51.*

2 ______ food does an elephant eat every day?
About *40/60/80* kg.

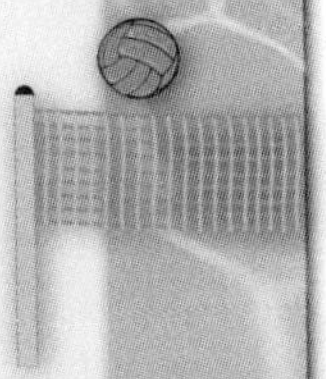

3 ______ people are there in a volleyball team?
There are *4/6/8.*

4 ______ is €50 in US dollars?
It's about *$20–$30/$60–$90/$130–$150.*

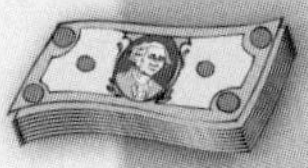

5 ______ milk does a cow produce every day?
About *10/20/30* litres.

6 ______ countries are there in the world?
There are about *105/145/195.*

7 ______ people live in the UK?
About *30/60/90* million.

8 ______ chocolate does each person in the USA eat a year?
About *5/10/15* kg.

some, any, a GRAMMAR 7.3

3 Colin has got a new flat in Tayford. Read the conversation. Then fill in the gaps with *some*, *any* or *a*.

COLIN Hi, Mum. I'm in my new home.
MUM Oh, good. Is there [1] *any* furniture?
COLIN Yes, in the living room there's [2] ______ big armchair and [3] ______ sofa, but there isn't [4] ______ TV. And in the kitchen there are [5] ______ chairs and [6] ______ small table, but there aren't [7] ______ cupboards.
MUM Have you got [8] ______ bed?
COLIN Yes, there's [9] ______ double bed – it's very comfortable. And there's also [10] ______ desk and [11] ______ bookcase, but there aren't [12] ______ shelves.
MUM And have you got [13] ______ food?
COLIN Well, I've got [14] ______ milk and bread.
MUM Is that all? Are there [15] ______ shops nearby?
COLIN Yes, there are [16] ______ shops near the station. Don't worry, Mum, everything's OK!

4 Change the incorrect words in bold.

1 I've got ~~**any**~~ *some* eggs.
2 I'd like **an** information, please.
3 Are there **a** nice restaurants near your house?
4 I haven't got **no** money.
5 There's **some** single bed in the bedroom.
6 Is there **a** furniture in your flat?
7 Has your house got **any** garden?
8 I haven't got **a** brothers or sisters.
9 There isn't **some** shower in the bathroom.
10 There's **any** milk in the fridge.

Review: questions

5 **a** Make questions with these words.

1 DVDs / How many / have / got / you ?
How many DVDs have you got?

2 brothers / Have / or sisters / got / any / you ?
______
______

3 your / are / family / people / How many / there / in ?
______
______

4 week / do / spend on / every / How much / you / food ?
______
______

5 your / house / there / Is / airport / an / near ?
______
______

6 house / bedrooms / there / your / are / How many / in ?
______
______

7 there / in / street / cafés / Are / nice / your / any ?
______
______

b Answer the questions for you.

At the shops

Shops VOCABULARY 7.3

1 Match the shops to the things you buy or do in them.

1 a supermarket — d	a bread
2 a bank	b shoes
3 a bookshop	c medicines (aspirin, etc.)
4 a chemist's	d food
5 a clothes shop	e meat
6 a post office	f books
7 a butcher's	g furniture, TVs, etc.
8 a baker's	h dresses, coats, etc.
9 a department store	i send letters
10 a shoe shop	j change money
11 a kiosk or a newsagent's	k newspapers, etc.

Things to buy VOCABULARY 7.4

2 Write the missing letters.

1 a *m a p*
2 s __ __ __ __ __
3 a c __ __ __ __
4 t __ __ __ __ __ __ __
5 a l __ __ __
6 a __ __ __ __ __ __ __
7 p __ __ __ __ __ __ __ __
8 a g __ __ __ __ __ b __ __ __
9 a s __ __ __ __ __ __ __ __
10 c __ __ __ __ __ __ __ __ __
11 a n __ __ __ __ __ __ __ __ __
12 c __ __ __ __ __ __ __ __ __ __

What sales assistants say REAL WORLD 7.1
What customers say REAL WORLD 7.2

3 **a** Read these conversations in two shops. Fill in the gaps with the phrases in the boxes.

~~Can I help~~	Would you like	how much are	
your receipt	I'll have	over there	that's all
Anything else	Have you got any	can I have	

SALES ASSISTANT Hi. 1 *Can I help* you?
CUSTOMER Yes, please. 2 ________ guide books for the UK?
SA Yes, we have. They're 3 ________ .
C Oh yes, I see. 4 ________ this one, please. And 5 ________ these postcards?
SA They're 50p each.
C OK, I'll have six postcards. And 6 ________ six stamps, please?
SA Of course. 7 ________ ?
C No, 8 ________ , thanks.
SA Right, that's £16.55, please. 9 ________ a bag?
C No, thanks. I've got one.
SA OK. Here's your change and 10 ________ .
C Thanks a lot. Bye.

Thanks for	do you sell	That's	pin number
Do you need	how much are	Would you like	
the first floor	the small ones	Here you are	

SALES ASSISTANT 11 ________ any help?
CUSTOMER Yes, 12 ________ these suitcases?
SA The big ones are £45 and 13 ________ are £35.
C OK. I'll have this big one, please.
SA Of course. 14 ________ anything else?
C Yes, 15 ________ umbrellas?
SA Yes, we do. They're on 16 ________ .
C Oh, OK. I'll buy this first.
SA Right. 17 ________ £45, please. Your 18 ________ , please. Thanks. 19 ________ . Your receipt's in the bag.
C Great. 20 ________ your help. Bye.

b Read the conversations again. What do the customers buy?

What to wear

Clothes VOCABULARY 7.5

1 Do the puzzle.

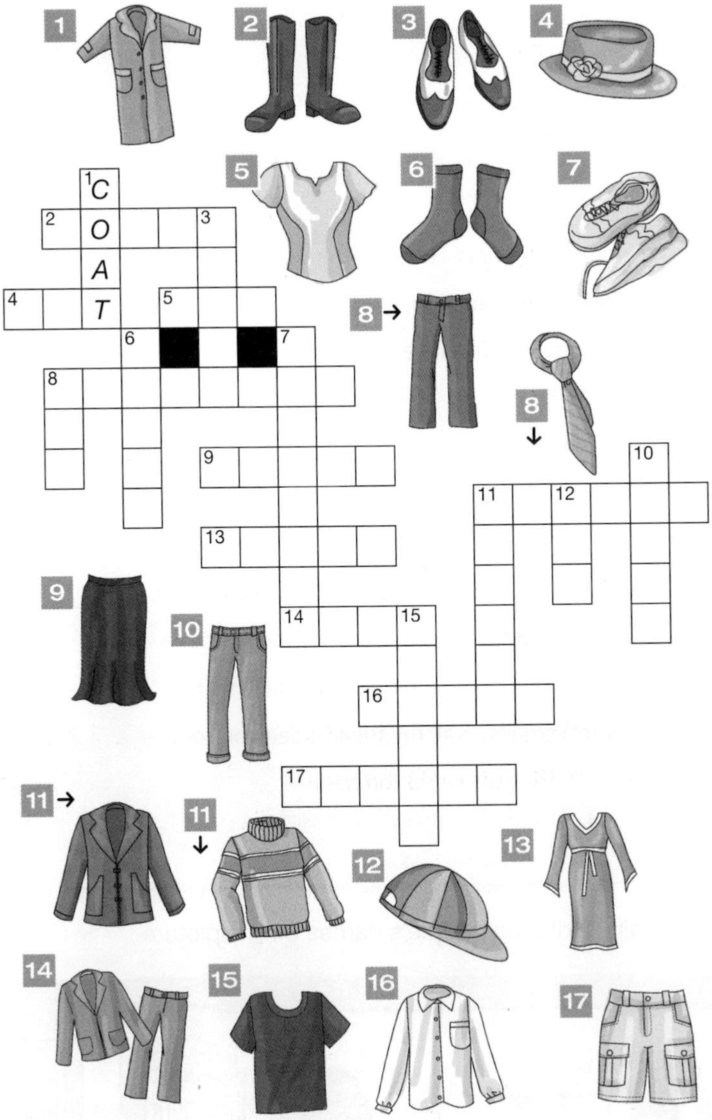

Plural nouns VOCABULARY 7.7

2 Correct these sentences.

1 Have you got ~~a~~ *any* black trousers?
2 My sister's got *a* new pair of boots.
3 I need a new shorts.
4 That's a nice pair of jean.
5 These clothes is very expensive.
6 There are a pair of shoe under the bed.
7 I haven't got a green trousers.

Reading

3 Read about Bluewater, a shopping centre in the UK. Are these sentences true (T) or false (F)?

1 [*T*] Bluewater is in England.
2 [ ] It's got over 330 clothes shops.
3 [ ] There are lots of different types of restaurants.
4 [ ] It's a good place to go for a special meal.
5 [ ] Bluewater is in the centre of a town.
6 [ ] There aren't any places to do sports there.
7 [ ] Bluewater is near London.
8 [ ] It's closed on Sundays.

www.thingstodointheuk.com

Things to do in the UK: Shopping

Bluewater, 5 miles from the town of Gravesend in England, is one of the biggest shopping centres in Europe.

There are over 330 shops, with over 100 clothes shops and three department stores. There are also over 50 cafés and restaurants with food from all over the world – American burgers, Italian pasta, South African chicken and, of course, traditional English fish and chips. Or for a special meal, there are also some excellent French, Spanish and Chinese restaurants with five-star food and service.

But Bluewater isn't only about shopping. It's in the middle of a beautiful park, with six lakes for boating and fishing. There's also a 13-screen cinema, a health club, a golf course, and lots of places for children to play. And when you're tired, there's a 'Place of Quiet' where you can go and relax.

Bluewater is only half an hour from the centre of London by train. There is also free parking for 13,000 cars. It is open every day, from 10 a.m.–9 p.m. from Monday to Friday, 9 a.m. – 9 p.m. on Saturdays and 11 a.m.–5 p.m. on Sundays.

Reading and Writing Portfolio 7 p76

Language Summary 8, Student's Book p145

Work VOCABULARY 8.1

1 a Fill in the gaps 1–6 with these verbs.

~~write~~	answer	take
sign	work	go to

1 *write*
a letter — an email
a *a report*

2 ______
at home — b ______
for a company

3 ______
notes — c ______

4 ______
a contract — d ______

5 ______
a meeting — e ______
work

6 ______
the phone — f ______

b Fill in gaps a–f with these words/phrases.

~~a report~~	a message
a conference	an email
a letter	in an office

Present Continuous: positive and negative GRAMMAR 8.1

2 a Read Nicola's email. Put the verbs in brackets in the correct form of the Present Continuous.

To: daniel.andrews@ukmail.co.uk

Hi Daniela

How are things? I hope you [1] *'re feeling* (feel) better now after your cold. I [2] ______ (sit) at my computer, but I [3] ______ (not work) very hard today! Usually our manager, Angela, watches us all the time – but at the moment she [4] ______ (visit) a customer, so we [5] ______ (not do) any work! Sue [6] ______ (not write) her report – she [7] ______ (look) for a cheap holiday on the internet. Sandra and Mia [8] ______ (not answer) their phones, they [9] ______ (read) magazines. Our accountant, Paul, [10] ______ (play) a computer game and my friend Emma [11] ______ (talk) to her boyfriend on the phone. And I [12] ______ (write) emails to all my friends! See you soon – I hope you [13] ______ (not work) too hard!

Love Nicola

b Read the email again. Write the people's names on the picture.

Present Continuous: questions and short answers

GRAMMAR 8.2

3 **a** Write the *yes/no* questions.

1 / Angela / visit / a customer? *Is Angela visiting a customer?*

2 / Sandra and Mia / read / magazines?

______

3 / they / answer / their phones?

______

4 / Sue / write / a report?

______

5 / Paul / play / a computer game?

______

6 / Emma / talk / to her boyfriend?

______

b Look again at the picture on p40. Then write short answers to the questions in **3a**.

1	*Yes, she is.*	3	______	5	______
2	______	4	______	6	______

4 **a** Make questions with these words.

1 doing / he / What / 's ?

What's he doing?

2 going / are / Where / you ?

______

3 watching / What / they / are ?

______

4 he / reading / 's / What ?

______

5 Who / is / waiting for / she ?

______

6 we / walking / are / Why / so fast ?

______

b Match these answers to the questions in **4a**.

a He's having dinner. *1*

b A car magazine.

c Because we're late.

d To the cinema.

e Her brother.

f An old film.

8B It's snowing

Types of transport

VOCABULARY 8.2

1 Do the puzzle. Find the type of transport (↓).

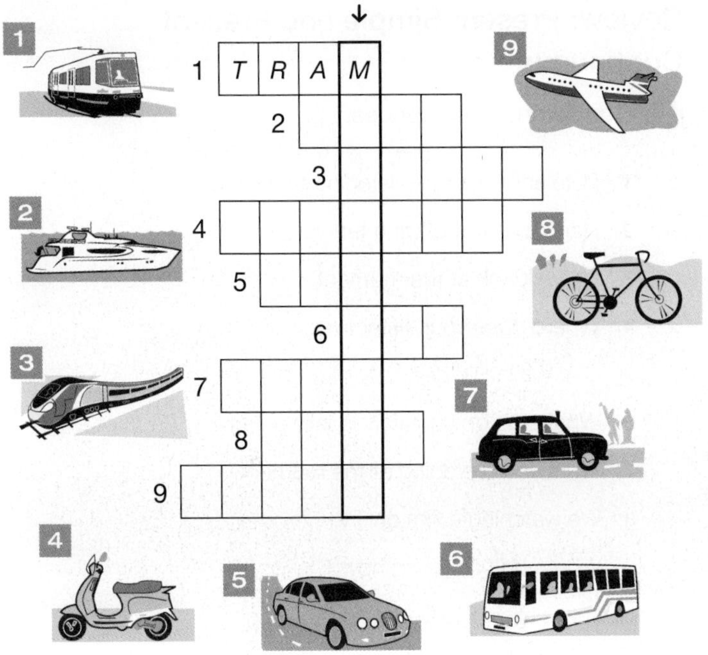

Travelling verbs and phrases

VOCABULARY 8.3

2 Write the sentences again with the correct form of these words/phrases.

~~take the coach~~ take the tube cycle fly drive walk

1 I went to Bath by coach.

I took the coach to Bath.

2 I always go to university by bike.

______

3 I came to school on foot today.

______

4 Did you go by tube?

______

5 We didn't go to Rome by car.

______

6 They usually go to New York by plane.

______

Present Simple or Present Continuous

GRAMMAR 8.3

3 Read what these people say about today's snow. Put the verbs in brackets in the Present Simple or Present Continuous.

MAX I usually [1] *work* (work) from 10 p.m. to 6 a.m. but I [2] *'m working* (work) today because of the snow. Normally I [3] __________ (not like) working in the day, but I [4] __________ (make) a lot of money today, so I'm very happy. I [5] __________ (drive) a businessman into town. He usually [6] __________ (take) the train, but he can't today, of course because there aren't any. The problem is, the traffic [7] __________ (not move) very fast!

JOE I usually [8] __________ (get up) about quarter to six and I [9] __________ (start) work at seven, but I [10] __________ (not work) today. The trains [11] __________ (not run) because of all the snow, so I [12] __________ (have) a day off. My wife, Judith, [13] __________ (work) at home every day and I [14] __________ (not see) her much in a normal week. At the moment Judith and I [15] __________ (walk) in the park – the trees are really beautiful in the snow.

BECKY AND GEORGE We [16] __________ (have) a fantastic day today! We normally [17] __________ (go) to school on a Thursday, of course, but our school is closed today because of the snow. At 11 o'clock we usually [18] __________ (have) an English class, but today we [19] __________ (make) a snowman in the garden! At the moment our mum [20] __________ (make) us our favourite lunch – sausages and chips. Yes, we [21] __________ (enjoy) the snow very much!

4 **a** Fill in the gaps with the correct form of the verbs in brackets.

1 When *does* Max usually *work* ? (work)
2 __________ he __________ a lot of money today? (make)
3 What __________ he __________ at the moment? (do)
4 What time __________ Joe usually __________ work? (start)
5 __________ he __________ today? (work)
6 What __________ Joe and Judith __________ at the moment? (do)
7 Which class __________ Becky and George usually __________ at 11 o'clock? (have)
8 What __________ they __________ at the moment? (do)
9 __________ they __________ the snow? (enjoy)

b Answer the questions in **4a**.

1 *At night.*
2 __________
3 __________
4 __________
5 __________
6 __________
7 __________
8 __________
9 __________

Review: Present Simple and Present Continuous

5 Correct these sentences.

1 Pete and Stacey ~~is~~ *are* listening to the radio.
2 Harry isn't like playing tennis.
3 I have lunch at the moment.
4 Where does your sister lives?
5 She live in Rio de Janeiro.
6 What time do Jennifer usually get up?
7 What you are doing at the moment?
8 We watching a film on TV.
9 Where do you going now?
10 I never going to bed before midnight.

On the phone

Reading

1 Match pictures A and B to the messages. Which message does not match a picture?

A

B

1 Hi. Andrew and Janine aren't in at the moment, but if you leave a message, we'll get back to you as soon as we can. Thanks for calling. Bye.

2 Thank you for calling the Filmworld Cinema. Please choose one of the following three options. For information about films showing this week, press 1. To book by credit card, press 2. For any other enquiries, press 3.

3 Hello, this is the voicemail of Tom Lenk at FTL Limited. I'm sorry, I can't take your call at the moment, but if you leave me a message I'll get back to you as soon as I can.

2 Read the messages again. Answer these questions.

1 Are Andrew and Janine at home now? ________

2 What do you do if you want to know the time of a film at Filmworld? ________

3 What number do you press to buy tickets? ________

4 Who works in an office? ________

Talking on the phone REAL WORLD 8.1

3 Tom is making some phone calls. Fill in the gaps with these phrases.

~~Is that~~ Can I call you back I'll call you later I'm calling call me on my mobile Speaking I'm in a meeting

1
TOM Hello. [1] *Is that* Mr Ali?
MR ALI [2] ________ .
TOM This is Tom Lenk. [3] ________ about the Richardson contract.
MR ALI I'm sorry, but [4] ________ at the moment. [5] ________ later?
TOM Yes, of course. I'm in the office until 5.30. After that you can [6] ________ .
MR ALI OK, [7] ________ . Bye.
TOM Goodbye.

can I speak to What time shall we meet I got your message Hold on a moment Can you It's Tom see you then

2
TOM Hello, [8] ________ Andrew, please?
JANINE [9] ________ , I'll get him.
ANDREW Hello?
TOM Hi, Andrew. [10] ________ . How are you?
ANDREW I'm fine, thanks. [11] ________ about the party.
TOM Good. [12] ________ come?
ANDREW Yes, of course. [13] ________ ?
TOM Let's meet at eight at my house. I'll drive.
ANDREW Fine, [14] ________ Bye.
TOM Bye.

Life outdoors

Indoor and outdoor activities VOCABULARY 8.4

1 Look at the pictures. Write sentences about things Laura can and can't do.

1 She can *sail*.
2 She can ______.
3 ______ Spanish.
4 ______.
5 ______.
6 She can't *surf*.
7 She can't ______.
8 ______.
9 ______.
10 ______.

Adjectives and adverbs VOCABULARY 8.5

2 Write the adverbs.

1	safe	*safely*	6	fast	______
2	happy	______	7	beautiful	______
3	fluent	______	8	bad	______
4	easy	______	9	good	______
5	hard	______	10	careful	______

3 Tick the correct sentences. Change the words in bold that are incorrect.

1 Kurt is a very **careful** driver. ✓
2 He's also a ~~**well**~~ *good* tennis player.
3 Brendan is a very **slowly** driver.
4 My sister plays the violin **beautiful**.
5 Sharon's parents are very **good** dancers.
6 My mother always walks very **quick**.
7 I'm very **happy** today!

Reading

4 a Ray is working at the South Wales Adventure Centre. Read his email to his family. Are these sentences true (T) or false (F)?

1 [*F*] Ray doesn't like his job.
2 [ ] He is with a group of very young children.
3 [ ] Some of the group speak very good English.
4 [ ] They went cycling two days ago.
5 [ ] They don't usually go out in the evenings.
6 [ ] Agnes works at the adventure centre.

To: mum&dad; julie; richard

Hi everyone

I'm having a really [1]*(good)/well* time in Wales. At the moment I'm the leader of a group of twelve teenagers from France. I can't speak French very [2]*good/well*, but some of the children can speak English quite [3]*fluent/fluently*. We all do something different every day. Yesterday we went cycling. It was very hot so we all cycled very [4]*slow/slowly*. But they all enjoyed it, I think. And last Saturday we went windsurfing. Nobody in the group knew how to windsurf, but they learned [5]*fast/fastly* and some of them were [6]*excellent/excellently*! In the evenings we usually play games and sing songs together in the centre – there's one girl in the group, Agnes, who can sing really [7]*beautiful/beautifully*. I love the job and I'm very [8]*happy/happily* here. See you next month!

Love Ray

b Read the email again. Choose the correct words 1–8.

Reading and Writing Portfolio 8 p78

Answer Key

Welcome!

1 2 my 3 Hi 4 I'm 5 Nice 6 meet 7 too 8 Goodbye/Bye 9 See 10 Monday 11 you 12 Bye/Goodbye

2 1 one 2 two 3 three 4 four 5 five 6 six 7 seven 8 eight 9 nine 10 ten 11 eleven 12 twelve 13 thirteen 14 fourteen 15 fifteen 16 sixteen 17 seventeen 18 eighteen 19 nineteen 20 twenty

3 2 Look at the board. 3 Listen and practise. 4 Work in groups. 5 Ask and answer the questions. 6 Do exercise 3 on your own. 7 Fill in the gaps. 8 Listen and check. 9 Open your book. 10 Look at the photo on page 17. 11 Work in pairs. 12 Match the words to the pictures.

4a A B C D E F G H I J K L M N O P Q R S T U V W X Y Z

b a b c d e f g h i j k l m n o p q r s t u v w x y z

5 2 a chair 3 a DVD player 4 a pen 5 a computer 6 a book 7 a table 8 a dictionary 9 a CD player 10 a pencil

6 2 first 3 It's 4 surname 5 How 6 spell 7 Welcome 8 class 9 Thank

7 2 Tuesday 3 Wednesday 4 Thursday 5 Friday 6 Saturday 7 Sunday

1A How are you?

1 2 How are you 3 I'm fine 4 thanks 5 this is 6 Nice to meet you 7 You too

2 2 Mexico 3 Brazil 4 Argentina 5 the UK 6 Germany 7 Poland 8 France 9 Spain 10 Italy 11 Turkey 12 Egypt 13 Russia 14 China 15 Japan 16 Australia

3 2 Mexican 3 Brazilian 4 Argentinian 5 British 6 German 7 Polish 8 French 9 Spanish 10 Italian 11 Turkish 12 Egyptian 13 Russian 14 Chinese 15 Japanese 16 Australian

4 2 You're in room 403. 3 He's American. 4 We're from Istanbul. 5 She's a teacher. 6 They're Italian. 7 It's in room C.

5 2 name 3 Where 4 from 5 I'm 6 What are 7 Our names 8 are you 9 We're 10 What are 11 His name's 12 her name's 13 Where are 14 They're

6 2 I 3 his 4 they 5 Her 6 their 7 He 8 your 9 she 10 We 11 your 12 our 13 It's 14 her

1B Coffee break

1 2 police officer 3 teacher 4 actor 5 builder 6 musician 7 waitress 8 sales assistant 9 cleaner 10 doctor ↓ accountant

2 2 an 3 a 4 an 5 a 6 a 7 an 8 a 9 an 10 a

3 2 We aren't from Poland. We're not from Poland. 3 You aren't late. You're not late. 4 I'm not retired. 5 They aren't from Rome. They're not from Rome. 6 She isn't an accountant. She's not an accountant. 7 Mark isn't unemployed. Mark's not unemployed.

4a 2 Is Penélope Cruz an actress? 3 Are George Clooney and Brad Pitt musicians? 4 Is Eric Clapton from England? 5 Are George Clooney and Brad Pitt from the USA? 6 Is Penélope Cruz from Italy?

b 2 Yes, she is. 3 No, they aren't./No, they're not. 4 Yes, he is. 5 Yes, they are. 6 No, she isn't./No, she's not.

5 2 not 3 from 4 job 5 a 6 an 7 am 8 me 9 No 10 from 11 do 12 a 13 an

1C Personal details

1 b thirty-three c forty-four d fifty-five e sixty-six f seventy-seven g eighty-eight h ninety-nine i a hundred

2 2 thirty-one 3 seventy-two 4 sixty-seven 5 twenty-eight 6 thirty-four 7 fifty-three 8 a hundred

3a b What's your first name? c How old are you? d Are you married? e What's your mobile number? f what's your email address? g What's your nationality? h what's your address? i What's your postcode? j What's your home number?

b A3 B1 C2

1D Lost property

1 2 wallet 3 suitcase 4 camera 5 umbrella 6 bike 7 shoes 8 ID card 9 laptop 10 dress 11 watch 12 mobile

2 2 watches 3 men 4 dresses 5 people 6 diaries 7 hotels 8 women 9 email addresses 10 children

3 2 That 3 that 4 this 5 That 6 these 7 Those 8 that

4 3 ✓ 4 ✓ 5 Evrim is from **Turkey**. 6 Marcelo's address is **22 High St, NW12 3WS**. 7 ✓ 8 ✓ 9 The class is in room **12**.

2A What's important?

1a 2 small 3 young 4 expensive 5 fast 6 beautiful 7 difficult 8 wrong 9 good 10 new

b 2 big 3 old 4 cheap 5 slow 6 ugly 7 easy 8 right 9 bad 10 old

c **across:** beautiful, cheap, easy, right, wrong, small, difficult, young, new, ugly, early **down:** big, good, expensive, old, fast, bad, late, slow

2 3 I've got a **new mobile**. 4 ✓ 5 These are **expensive** shoes. 6 Steve's got a **very old car**. 7 ✓ 8 They've got three **big** dogs.

3 2 hasn't got 3 's got 4 's got 5 hasn't got 6 's got 7 have got 8 've got 9 haven't got

4 2 Has Carl got a laptop? 3 Have Jack and Lucy got a camera? 4 Has Linda got a mobile? 5 Has Carl got a DVD player? 6 Have Jack and Lucy got a mobile?

5 2 No, he hasn't. 3 No, they haven't. 4 Yes, she has. 5 Yes, he has. 6 Yes, they have.

2B The Browns

1 1 Arthur 2 Shirley 4 Brenda 5 Nate 6 George 7 Tracy 8 David

2 2 grandmother 3 uncle 4 aunt 5 grandchildren 6 granddaughter 7 grandsons 8 cousins 9 grandparents

3 2 Brenda's 3 Shirley's 4 George's 5 Terry's 6 David's 7 Brenda's 8 Nate's

4a 2 Terry's unemployed at the moment. 3 Megan is Terry's wife. 4 She's got a new laptop. 5 Nate is Brenda's husband. 6 He's a doctor.

b 2 is 3 possessive 4 has 5 possessive 6 is

5a 2 How many brothers and sisters has Terry got? 3 Who is Tracy and David's grandfather? 4 How many children has Brenda got? 5 Who are Terry and Brenda's parents? 6 How many grandchildren have Arthur and Shirley got? 7 Who is David and Tracy's uncle? 8 How many children have Terry and Megan got?

b 2 One. 3 Arthur. 4 Two.

5 Arthur and Shirley 6 Three. 7 Terry. 8 One.

2C Time and money

1 1 One year = 12 months = 52 weeks = 365 days. 2 One day = 24 hours = 1,440 minutes = 86,400 seconds.

2 2 (a) quarter past three; three fifteen 3 half past seven; seven thirty 4 (a) quarter to four; three forty-five 5 ten to nine; eight fifty 6 twelve o'clock; midnight

3 2 past 3 time 4 at 5 What 6 from 7 to 8 Have 9 the 10 it's 11 Thanks 12 welcome

4 2 Can I have two tickets 3 Yes, please. How much is that? 4 Here you are. 5 What time is the film? 6 Right. Thanks a lot. 7 Thanks. Bye.

2D Where's the baby?

1 2 a mirror 3 curtains 4 a window 5 a bookcase 6 a plant 7 a desk 8 a sofa 9 a lamp 10 a coffee table 11 a carpet 12 the floor

2 2 It's behind the sofa. 3 It's under the coffee table. 4 They're on the coffee table. 5 It's in front of the TV. 6 They're in the suitcase.

3 2 Yes, they are. 3 Three. 4 Two. (Barry and Liz) 5 No, it isn't. 6 No, they haven't. 7 Yes, they have. 8 No, they haven't.

4 2 beautiful 3 difficult 4 small 5 manager 6 waitress 7 camera 8 wallet 9 umbrella 10 address

3A My day

1 2 live 3 to bed 4 lunch 5 home 6 bed

2 2 I have breakfast at half past eight/eight thirty. 3 I leave home at (a) quarter past nine/nine fifteen. 4 I start classes at ten o'clock. 5 I have lunch at half past twelve/twelve thirty in the university café. 6 I finish classes at half past five/five thirty. 7 I get home at (a) quarter past six/six fifteen. 8 I have dinner at half past seven/seven thirty. 9 I go to bed at 12 o'clock/midnight.

3 2 in 3 at 4 from 5 from 6 for 7 in 8 in 9 at 10 at 11 for 12 from, to

4 2 my 3 they 4 their 5 her 6 she 7 you 8 your 9 he 10 his 11 our 12 We

5 2 get up 3 have breakfast 4 have lunch 5 start work 6 finish work 7 have dinner 8 get home 9 go to bed 10 sleep

6 2 What time do they get up? 3 Where do they have lunch? 4 What time/When do they leave home? 5 Where do they have dinner? 6 What time/When do they get home? 7 What do they do after they get home? 8 What time/When do they go to bed?

3B Free time

1 2 out 3 with 4 watch 5 to 6 out 7 stay 8 go 9 sport 10 friends

2 b phone friends c have coffee with friends d watch TV e go to concerts f go shopping

3 2 every 3 at 4 in 5 in 6 every 7 on 8 at 9 at 10 On 11 in 12 Every 13 at 14 at

4 3 They don't get home at seven in the evening. 4 They don't go out a lot in the week. 5 ✓ 6 They don't get up early at the weekend. 7 ✓

5 2 Do your parents work? No, they don't. 3 Do you go shopping on Saturdays? Yes, I do./Yes, we do. 4 Do we finish work at five o'clock? No, you don't./No, we don't. 5 Do they go to the cinema a lot? Yes, they do. 6 Do you go to concerts at the weekend? Yes, I do./Yes, we do.

6a 2g 3e 4d 5h 6c 7a 8b

b 2 No, she isn't./No, she's not. 3 No, he hasn't. 4 No, I don't./No, we don't. 5 No, they aren't./No, they're not. 6 No, you don't./No, we don't. 7 No, I'm not. 8 No, they don't.

3C Special days

1 b 8 August c 11 November d 4 April e 9 September f 5 May g 2 February h 10 October i 6 June j 3 March k 12 December l 7 July

2 a 2 1st January 1987 3 14th May 1971 4 23rd July 2012 5 2nd February 2005

b 2 What's the date tomorrow? 3 When's your birthday? 4 When's your mother's birthday?

3 1 Happy birthday! 2 Happy New Year! 3 Happy anniversary! 4 Congratulations!

4 2 on the twenty-fifth 3 What shall we 4 Why don't we 5 I don't think so 6 What about 7 Maybe 8 Let's 9 that's a good idea

3D Early bird?

1 2 usually 3 never 4 often 5 always 6 never 7 hardly ever

2 2 We're **usually** at home on Sunday evenings. 3 They **often** go to bed after midnight. 4 I'm **always** tired on Monday mornings. 5 I **sometimes** do sport on Saturdays. 6 I **usually** have a party on my birthday. 7 My children **hardly ever** get up early at the weekend. 8 They're **never** at home on New Year's Eve.

3 2 Two, a/one brother and a/one sister. 3 In California. 4 Yes, she is. 5 Five. (Ray, his parents, Peter and Jeanette) 6 On the fourth Thursday in November.

4 2 Ray's mother/mum 3 Peter 4 Peter and Jeanette 5 Peter and Jeanette 6 Ray and his parents 7 Thanksgiving 8 Ray and his family

4A Away from home

1 2 go 3 go 4 listen 5 play 6 listen 7 watch 8 go 9 go 10 play 11 go 12 read 13 take

2 3 ✓ 4 she watches 5 ✓ 6 it goes 7 he teaches 8 ✓ 9 it has 10 she studies

3 2 go 3 lives 4 eat 5 gets 6 go

4a 2 works 3 speaks 4 goes 5 Gabriela lives in Bogotá, Colombia. 6 She teaches Spanish. 7 She speaks very good English. 8 In her free time she plays tennis.

b 2 Silvio doesn't live in London. 3 Silvio doesn't work in a language school. 4 Silvio and Gabriela don't live in Turkey. 5 Silvio and Gabriela don't speak Chinese. 6 Gabriela doesn't teach English.

5 2 doesn't have 3 starts 4 finishes 5 go 6 get up 7 have 8 get 9 doesn't have 10 has 11 gets 12 watches 13 does 14 like 15 don't like 16 see

4B First Date!

1 2 fast food 3 video games 4 rock music 5 cooking 6 shopping for clothes 7 travelling 8 Chinese food

2a 2 really 3 like 4 quite 5 OK 6 don't 7 hate

b 2 doesn't like 3 quite likes 4 is OK 5 likes 6 loves 7 hates

3 2 Does she teach French? Yes, she

does. 3 Does she listen to dance music? Yes, she does. 4 Does she like cooking? No, she doesn't. 5 Does Hugo live in Bristol? Yes, he does. 6 Does he work in a school? No, he doesn't. 7 Does he like fast food? No, he doesn't. 8 Does he watch a lot of DVDs? Yes, he does.

4a 2 What does she do in her free time? 3 What music does she like? 4 When does she play tennis? 5 What food does she like? 6 When does she go clubbing?

b b3 c1 d4 e6 f2

5 2 Where does he live? 3 What music does he like? 4 What food does he like? 5 What does he do in his free time? 6 When does he go cycling?

4C Eating out

1 2 a burger and chips 3 a pizza 4 a chicken salad 5 a bottle of beer 6 a glass of red wine 7 a bottle of mineral water 8 a cup of coffee

2a 2 Yes, we'd **like** two **pizzas**, please. 3 **Would** you like anything **else**? 4 **Can** I have a mixed **salad**, please? 5 **What** would you like to **drink**? 6 **I'd** like a beer, **please**. 7 **Would** you like **tea** or coffee? 8 No, thanks. **Can** we have the **bill**, please?

b 2C 3W 4C 5W 6C 7W 8C

3a 2 Yes, I'd like the burger and chips, please. 3 And can I have the tuna salad, please? 4 What would you like to drink? 5 We'd like a bottle of red wine. 6 Would you like a dessert? 7 Yes, can I have the apple pie? 8 And I'd like the fruit salad, please. 9 Would you like anything else? 10 Yes, two coffees, please. 11 And can we have the bill, please?

b They order the burger and chips, the tuna salad, a bottle of red wine, the apple pie, the fruit salad and two coffees.

4D Breakfast time

1 2 sausages 3 orange juice 4 bread 5 red wine 6 biscuits 7 cereal 8 fish 9 vegetables 10 eggs ↓ sandwiches

2 2 – ; – 3 an ; a 4 – ; – 5 a 6 – ; – 7 a 8 a ; – 9 – ; – 10 a ; –

3 2T 3F 4F 5T 6F

5A Three generations

1a 2 quiet, noisy 3 boring, interesting 4 friendly, unfriendly 5 tall, short 6 happy, unhappy 7 well, ill 8 lucky, unlucky 9 hot, cold 10 fantastic, awful 11 amazing, terrible

b 2 short 3 hot 4 tall 5 ill 6 well 7 unhappy 8 short

2 2 was 3 were 4 were 5 was 6 wasn't 7 were 8 was 9 wasn't 10 were 11 was 12 was

3a 2 Were Matt and Andy in the same class? 3 Was Matt in the USA in 1992? 4 Was the party at Matt and Andy's hotel? 5 Was Penny very friendly at first? 6 Were Matt and Penny married in 1994? 7 Was Jason born in Bristol? 8 Was it Matt's birthday yesterday?

b 2 Yes, they were. 3 No, he wasn't. 4 Yes, it was. 5 No, she wasn't. 6 No, they weren't. 7 Yes, he was. 8 Yes, it was.

4 2 When was 3 Who was 4 When was 5 What were 6 How old was

5B Famous films

1 2 make 3 meet 4 get 5 write 6 study 7 have 8 move 9 win 10 become 11 win 12 move 13 study 14 get 15 become 16 have 17 meet 18 leave 19 write 20 make

2a 2 started 3 visited 4 loved 5 studied 6 looked 7 lived 8 worked 9 married 10 wanted 11 liked 12 stopped

b 2 got 3 became 4 won 5 met, went 6 left, wrote 7 made, was

3 2 moved 3 studied 4 wanted 5 made 6 became 7 was 8 met 9 got 10 was 11 changed 12 was 13 studied 14 became 15 won 16 made 17 married

4 2 When **did** he **move** to the USA? 3 **When did** he **make** the first *Terminator* film? 4 **How many** years **was** he Governor of California? 5 **Who did** he **get** married to in 1986? 6 **When was** Sigourney Weaver **born**? 7 **When did** she **change** her name? 8 **What did** she **study** at Stanford University? 9 **When did** she **win** an Oscar? 10 **How many** *Alien* films **did** she **make**?

5a 2 did, were 3 Were 4 did 5 was 6 did 7 did, was 8 Was 9 did 10 did

5C Four weekends

1 2 cleaned 3 did 4 cleaned 5 went for 6 was 7 got 8 went to 9 had 10 went for 11 had 12 stayed 13 watched 14 went to 15 wrote 16 did 17 wrote 18 watched

2a 2 Wow! 3 Oh, nice. 4 Oh, dear. 5 What a shame. 6 Oh, right.

b b What was it like? c Who did you go with? d What did you do there? e Where did you stay? f What did you do on Saturday evening? g What did you see?

5D Competitions

1

S	E	C	R	E	X	C	I	T	E	D
B	O	R	E	D	O	R	I	C	H	E
U	C	O	E	M	P	T	Y	P	L	A
S	H	W	Q	F	A	M	T	O	X	P
Y	I	D	A	N	G	E	R	O	U	S
C	L	E	A	N	M	L	E	R	E	A
T	J	D	I	R	T	Y	R	A	U	F
C	O	M	F	O	R	T	A	B	L	E

2a 2 very 3 quite 4 really 5 too 6 really 7 too

b 1D 2C 3A 4B

3a 3 to 4 was 5 very/really 6 walked 7 went 8 very/really 9 had 10 was 11 in 12 were 13 him 14 arrrived 15 at

b 3 on Saturday afternoon 4 on Sunday morning 5 on Saturday afternoon 6 on Saturday evening 7 (at about midnight) on Sunday 8 last June

6A Google it!

1 2 went 3 reading 4 have 5 download 6 chats 7 use 8 download 9 have 10 sent; get

2 2 was 3 worked 4 went 5 studied 6 left 7 worked 8 wanted 9 had 10 were 11 called 12 changed 13 sold 14 had 15 sold 16 started

3 3 ✓ 4 He didn't work in Los Angeles. 5 He didn't have the idea for Amazon on a plane. 6 Amazon wasn't the first name for the website. 7 ✓ 8 The website didn't start selling CDs in 1996.

4 2 Did Jeff Bezos go to Princeton University 3 Did he study physics at university? 4 Did he have the idea for Amazon in the car? 5 Was Cadabra the first name for the website?

6 Did Amazon sell its first book in June 1995? 7 Did Amazon start selling CDs in 1998?

5 2 Yes, he did. 3 No, he didn't. 4 Yes, he did. 5 Yes, it was. 6 No, it didn't. 7 Yes, it did.

6 2 Where **were** you born? 3 What time did you **start** work? 4 He **stopped** work at ten last night. 5 Where **were** they last night? 6 I didn't **watch** TV yesterday. 7 Where **was he** born? 8 I **didn't play** tennis last weekend.

6B Changing technology

1 2 TV programme 3 turn on 4 turn off 5 battery 6 get 7 channel 8 apps 9 record 10 charge 11 GPS

2 2 last 3 ago 4 in 5 last 6 in 7 ago 8 last 9 in 10 last 11 ago 12 ago

3 2 could; could; can 3 could; couldn't; can 4 couldn't; can; can 5 can; can; can't

4 2 Could you **record** programmes in 1974? 3 Can I **charge** my phone here, please? 4 Can you download videos **onto** your laptop? 5 I can ~~to~~ watch TV on my mobile. 6 I met him about six years **ago**. 7 My parents went to Spain **in** 2010. 8 I didn't **get** a text from you yesterday. 9 Did you sister **call** you last night? 10 I often chat **to/with** my friends online. 11 I **was born** in Buenos Aires. 12 We went to the cinema **last weekend**.

5 1b No, they can't. 2 No, he can't. 3 No, she can't. 4 Yes, they can. 5a Yes, he can. b No, he can't. 6a Yes, he can. b No, he can't. 7 No, they can't. 8 No, they can't.

6C The news

1 2 bought I 3 crashed R 4 said I 5 told I 6 saved R 7 received R 8 found I 9 lost I 10 sailed R 11 put I 12 died R

2a A2 B3 C1

b 2 In his wallet. 3 7.38 a.m. 4 About a thousand. 5 Twentyfourseven. 6 Two hundred.

3 2 No, where was it? 3 Oh no, that's terrible. 4 Really? 5 Is she OK? 6 Oh, that's good. 7 Did you read about 8 No, what happened? 9 You're joking!

6D Mario Man

1 2 a 3 a 4 a 5 the 6 the 7 the 8 The 9 the 10 the 11 the 12 the 13 The 14 a

2a 2 the 3 a 4 the 5 an 6 a 7 an 8 the; the; the 9 the 10 a

b **1–3 yes answers:** You probably don't have much time to study. Try to do one different thing from the list every week.

4–7 yes answers: You like learning English and you know that studying outside class is good practice. Maybe you can choose on thing from the list to do at the weekend.

8–10 yes answers: You love learning English and you probably do lots of things in English outside class. Congratulations!

3 2 at 3 for 4 from 5 on 6 for 7 at 8 with 9 in 10 to 11 in 12 on 13 to 14 on 15 in 16 for

4 2 favourite 3 January 4 eighteen 5 different 6 friendly 7 dangerous 8 biscuits 9 daughter 10 crowded 11 swimming 12 divorced 13 vegetables 14 grandfather 15 shopping 16 Wednesday 17 chocolate 18 interesting 19 birthday 20 tomatoes

7A Where I live

1 a hotel 10 a station 1 houses 3 flats 2 a road 12 a market 11 a square 5 a café 6 shops 7 a bus station 4 a park 9

2 2 there's 3 There are 4 There are 5 there's 6 there isn't 7 There are 8 there aren't 9 There's 10 there isn't 11 There's 12 There's 13 there isn't

3 2 Are there any museums? No, there aren't. 3 Is there a park? Yes, there is. 4 Are there any flats? Yes, there are. 5 Is there a cinema? No, there isn't. 6 Are there any restaurants? Yes, there are. 7 Is there an airport? No there isn't. 8 Is there a bus station? Yes, there is.

4 2 It isn't 3 there are 4 There are 5 there's 6 there are 7 They aren't 8 It's 9 There are 10 it's 11 There are 12 they're

5 2 Colin hasn't got a new car. 3 His sister doesn't work in Tayford. 4 Their parents don't live in London. 5 They haven't got a big house. 6 They didn't go to Oxford last year. 7 Colin's grandparents weren't doctors. 8 Brenda wasn't born in Tayford.

7B A new home

1 2 sofa 3 desk 4 chair 5 fridge 6 plant 7 single bed 8 armchair 9 table 10 coooker 11 bath 12 toilet 13 sink 14 double bed ↓ washing machine

2 2 How much; 80 3 How many; 6 4 How much; $60–$90 5 How much; 30 6 How many; 195 7 How many; 60 8 How much; 10

3 2 a 3 a 4 a 5 some 6 a 7 any 8 a 9 a 10 a 11 a 12 any 13 any 14 some 15 any 16 some

4 2 I'd like **some** information, please. 3 Are there **any** nice cafés near your house? 4 I haven't got **any** money. 5 There's **a** single bed in the bedroom. 6 Is there **any** furniture in your flat? 7 Has your house got **a** garden? 8 I haven't got **any** brothers or sisters. 9 There isn't **a** shower in the bathroom. 10 There's **some** milk in the fridge.

5a 2 Have you got any brothers or sisters? 3 How many people are there in your family? 4 How much do you spend every week on food? 5 Is there an airport near your house? 6 How many bedrooms are there in your house? 7 Are there any nice cafés in your street?

7C At the shops

1 2j 3f 4c 5h 6i 7e 8a 9g 10b 11k

2 2 stamps 3 a cake 4 tissues 5 a lamp 6 aspirin 7 postcards 8 a guide book 9 a suitcase 10 chocolate 11 a newspaper 12 cigarettes

3a 2 Have you got any 3 over there 4 I'll have 5 how much are 6 can I have 7 Anything else 8 that's all 9 Would you like 10 your receipt 11 Do you need 12 How much are 13 the small ones 14 Would you like 15 Do you sell 16 the first floor 17 That's 18 pin number 19 Here you are 20 Thanks for

b A A guidebook, six postcards and six stamps. B A big suitcase.

7D What to wear

1 2 boots 3 shoes 4 hat 5 top 6 socks 7 trainers 8 → trousers 8 ↓ tie 9 skirt 10 jeans 11 → jacket 11 ↓ jumper 12 cap 13 dress 14 suit 15 T-shirt 16 shirt 17 shorts

2 3 I need **some** new shorts./I need a new **pair of** shorts. 4 That's a nice pair of **jeans**. 5 These clothes **are** very expensive. 6 There's/There **is** a pair of shoes under the bed.
7 I haven't got **any** green trousers./ I haven't got a **pair of** green trousers.

3 2F 3T 4T 5F 6F 7T 8F

8A The meeting

1a 2 work 3 take 4 sign 5 go to 6 answer

b b in an office c a message d a letter e a conference f an email/a letter

2a 2 'm sitting 3 'm not working 4 's visiting 5 aren't doing/'re not doing 6 isn't writing/'s not writing 7 's looking 8 aren't answering/'re not answering 9 're reading 10 's playing 11 's talking 12 'm writing 13 aren't working/'re not working

b a Paul b Sue c Emma e Mia

3a 2 Are Sandra and Mia reading magazines? 3 Are they answering their phones? 4 Is Sue writing a report? 5 Is Paul playing a computer game? 6 Is Emma talking to her boyfriend?

b 2 Yes, they are. 3 No, they aren't./ No, they're not. 4 No, she isn't./ No, she's not. 5 Yes, he is. 6 Yes, she is.

4a 2 Where are you going? 3 What are they watching? 4 What's he reading? 5 Who is she waiting for? 6 Why are we walking so fast?

b b4 c6 d2 e5 f3

8B It's snowing!

1 2 boat 3 train 4 scooter 5 car 6 bus 7 taxi 8 bike 9 plane ↓ motorbike

2 2 I always cycle to university. 3 I walked to school today. 4 Did you take the tube? 5 We didn't drive to Rome. 6 They usually fly to New York.

3 3 don't like 4 'm making 5 'm driving 6 takes 7 isn't moving/ 's not moving 8 get up 9 start 10 'm not working 11 aren't running 12 'm having 13 works 14 don't see 15 are walking 16 're having 17 go 18 have 19 're making 20 's making 21 're enjoying

4a 2 Is ... making 3 's/is ... doing 4 does ... start 5 Is ... working 6 are ... doing 7 do ... have 8 are .... doing 9 Are ... enjoying

b 2 Yes, he is. 3 He's driving a businessman into town. 4 At 7.00. 5 No, he isn't./No, he's not. 6 They're walking in the park. 7 English. 8 They're making a snowman. 9 Yes, they are.

5 2 Harry **doesn't** like playing tennis. 3 **I'm having** lunch at the moment. 4 Where does your sister **live?** 5 She **lives** in Rio de Janeiro. 6 What time **does** Jennifer usually get up? 7 What **are you** doing at the moment? 8 We**'re** watching a film on TV. 9 Where **are** you going now? 10 I never **go** to bed before midnight.

8C On the phone

1 A3 B1
Message 2 doesn't match a picture.

2 1 No, they aren't./No, they're not. 2 You press 1. 3 You press 2. 4 Tom Lenk.

3 2 Speaking 3 I'm calling 4 I'm in a meeting 5 Can I call you back 6 call me on my mobile 7 I'll call you later 8 can I speak to 9 Hold on a moment 10 It's Tom 11 I got your message 12 Can you 13 What time shall we meet 14 see you then

8D Life outdoors

1 2 ski 3 She can speak Spanish. 4 She can ride a horse. 5 She can cook. 7 She can't drive. 8 She can't sing. 9 She can't ride a motorbike. 10 She can't play a musical instrument./She can't play the violin.

2 2 happily 3 fluently 4 easily 5 hard 6 fast 7 beautifully 8 badly 9 well 10 carefully

3 3 Brendan is a very **slow** driver. 4 My sister plays the violin **beautifully.** 5 ✓ 6 My mother always walks very **quickly.** 7 ✓

4a 2F 3T 4F 5T 6F

b 2 well 3 fluently 4 slowly 5 fast 6 excellent 7 beautifully 8 happy

9A Holiday South Africa

1 2 have a picnic 3 go diving 4 go camping 5 go to museums 6 rent a car 7 go on a boat trip 8 stay in a hotel 9 go sightseeing 10 go to the beach 11 go on a guided tour 12 travel by public transport

2 3 went on 4 had 5 went on 6 went to 7 went to 8 go 9 travel by 10 rented 11 went 12 go on

3 2 Tourists go to Sydney to visit the Opera House. 3 A lot of people come to London to study English. 4 I went to New York to stay with an old friend. 5 I went to the butcher's to buy some meat. 6 We're going to the park to have a picnic.

4 3 He flew to New York ~~for~~ to see his cousin. 4 ✓ 5 I need £100 **to** buy a camera. 6 ✓ 7 ✓ 8 Gary drove to Brighton to **visit** some friends. 9 We went to the market ~~for~~ to buy a carpet. 10 ✓

9B A trip to Egypt

1 2 a mountain 3 an island 4 the desert 5 a forest 6 the countryside 7 a river 8 a hill 9 a lake 10 a wood

2 2 Juliet looks younger than Patrick. 3 Patrick is hotter than Juliet. 4 Patrick's suitcase is bigger than Juliet's. 5 Juliet looks happier than Patrick. 6 Patrick had a worse time than Juliet. 7 Juliet had a better time than Patrick.

3 2 The Ritz is bigger than Raffles. 3 Raffles is smaller. 4 Rooms at Raffles are cheaper than rooms at the Ritz. 5 The Ritz is more expensive. 6 Raffles is nearer to the airport. 7 It's easier to decide where to eat at the Ritz. 8 It's more difficult to decide where to eat at Raffles. 9 You can have dinner earlier at The Ritz. 10 I think The Ritz/Raffles looks more beautiful than Raffles/The Ritz.

9C A day out

1a 1C 2A 3B

b 2 Bournemouth 3 Stratford and Bath 4 Bournemouth and Stratford 5 Bournemouth 6 Stratford and Bath 7 Stratford

2a They decide to go to Bath.

b 2 to go 3 go 4 see 5 go 6 to go 7 sit 8 go 9 to go 10 visit 11 do 12 stay 13 to drive 14 take 15 go

Answer Key

3

Q	R	A	B	B	I	T	A	V	U	G
M	O	U	Z	K	L	I	O	N	S	O
O	Y	L	B	S	T	G	S	M	H	R
N	C	H	I	C	K	E	N	O	E	I
K	O	G	R	E	A	R	A	U	E	L
E	W	B	D	R	W	I	K	S	P	L
Y	W	O	L	F	O	M	E	E	B	A

9D Time for a change

1 2 revising 3 to buy 4 to go 5 watching 6 to go 7 staying 8 to visit 9 to sign 10 smoking

2a 2T 3F 4F 5T 6F

b 2 working 3 being 4 to live 5 living 6 to learn 7 studying 8 to become 9 to move 10 to learn 11 living 12 to go 13 writing 14 to write 15 having 16 to live 17 to stay

10A Stay fit and healthy

1 2 take 3 do 4 wash 5 carry 6 have 7 spend 8 get 9 spent 10 get 11 get off 12 take 13 wash 14 do 15 spent

2 2 Katrina and Alex play tennis once a week. 3 We go to the supermarket every week. 4 You should take some aspirin twice a day. 5 I have an English class three times a week. 6 We go to the theatre every three months. 7 My parents always go on holiday three times a year.

3 2 How often **do** you go clubbing? 3 He goes to the gym every **week**. 4 I go to the doctor **twice** a year. 5 How often **does** he play football? 6 I study Spanish three **times** a week. 7 She visits her parents **every week**. 8 I phone my mum **once** a day.

4 1 Use 2 Don't walk 3 Open 4 don't touch 5 break

5a 2 shouldn't be 3 should go 4 should study 5 should do 6 shouldn't talk 7 should ask 8 shouldn't sleep

10B What's she like?

1 Across 3 good-looking 5 slim 8 blonde 12 bald 13 overweight 15 shy 16 grey 18 middle-aged Down 2 funny 4 kind 6 lazy 7 moustache 8 beard 9 outgoing 10 short 11 selfish 14 generous 17 young

2a 2 What does he look like? 3 What does he like doing? 4 What's he like? 5 How are you?

b a How are you? b What's he like? c What does he look like? d What does he like doing? e What's his name?

3a 2 was 3 was 4 's 5 's got 6 's 7 've got 8 was 9 's 10 's got 11 was 12 's 13 's got 14 's 15 was 16 was 17 's got 18 's 19 's 20 've got

b 2 Lily 3 Adriana 4 Lily 5 Adriana 6 Natalia 7 Adriana

10C I feel ill

1 1 temperature 2 headache; sore throat 3 cough; back 4 stomach ache; sick 5 hurts; toothache 6 terrible; cold

2 2 go **to the** dentist 3 go **to the** doctor 4 go home (–) 5 stay **in** bed 6 stay **at** home 7 take **some** antibiotics 8 take **the** day **off** 9 take **some** cough medicine 10 take **some** painkillers

3 2 feel very well 3 What's wrong 4 I've got 5 You shouldn't 6 the day off 7 get better soon 8 Are you alright 9 I feel terrible 10 the matter 11 I've got 12 feel sick 13 Why don't you 14 go to the doctor 15 Get well

10D Winter blues

1 2 It's windy in Chicago. 3 It's raining in London. 4 It's snowing in Moscow. 5 It's warm/20°C in Tokyo. 6 It's foggy in Bangkok. 7 It's hot/38°C in São Paolo. 8 It's cloudy in Melbourne.

2 2 rain 3 sunny 4 cloud 5 rain 6 snows 7 windy 8 wind 8 snow 10 foggy

3a 2T 3F 4T 5F 6T

b Spring, summer and winter are in the text. Autumn isn't in the text.

4 2 We **don't** like living here because **it's** too cold. 3 You **shouldn't** phone when the **baby's** sleeping. 4 We **didn't** see it because we **weren't** there. 5 **They've** got three TVs, but two **don't** work. 6 **Matt's** sure he **wasn't** at the meeting. 7 **I'd** like to move to Spain, but my wife **doesn't** want to.

11A Happy New Year!

1 2 house 3 weight 4 a holiday 5 smoking 6 a new job 7 fun 8 sweet things

2 2 isn't going to clean/'s not going to clean 3 's going to do 4 isn't going to meet/'s not going to meet 5 's going to clean 6 isn't going to do/'s not going to do 7 aren't going to meet 8 're going to clean 9 aren't going to do 10 are going (to go)

3 2 He's going to clean the car. 3 She's going to have a baby. 4 They're going to play tennis. 5 He's going to get a taxi. 6 It's going to rain.

4 2 What are you going to do there? 3 Where are you going to study? 4 What's your son going to do in the summer? 5 Where's he going to stay? 6 What are you going to see? 7 What are you going to do after the film? 8 Where are you going to be?

11B No more exams!

1 2 to get 3 take 4 passed 5 'm revising 6 failed 7 did 8 got 9 got 10 left 11 go

2 3 might 4 'm ... going to 5 'm going to 6 are ... going to 7 might 8 are going to 9 might 10 might

3a 2 Is he going to meet some friends in a bar? 3 Is he going to meet Carla this evening? 4 Is Carla going to a concert this weekend? 5 Are Austin and his brother going to Wales this weekend? 6 Are they going to stay in a hotel?

b 3 No, he isn't./No, he's not. 4 She might. 5 Yes, they are. 6 They might.

4 2 We might ~~to~~ come and visit you this evening. 3 We're going **to** have dinner on Sunday. 4 **Amanda's** going to move to Australia next year. 5 Tim **might** go to the theatre this evening. 6 Sid and Clare **are** going to study in the USA. 7 My brother might **study** engineering.

11C Directions

1a 2 on 3 Go 4 past 5 on 6 Do 7 turn 8 over 9 on 10 Is 11 near 12 in 13 along 14 on 15 can't

b 1 The hospital is number 3. 2 The Cordelia Hotel is number 6. 3 The café is number 5.

2 2 turn right 3 go past 4 opposite 5 Go over 6 next to 7 turn left 8 go over 9 past 10 Turn left 11 on your/the 12 opposite

11D An invitation

1 2 book 3 get 4 book 5 get 6 stay 7 rent 8 get 9 stay 10 book 11 get 12 book

2 **have** a great time; a bad cold; a bath; a shower **do** your homework; the housework; the washing; some exercise **go** swimming; sightseeing; clubbing; cycling **go to** the gym; the beach; the doctor; the dentist

3 2 Las Vegas. 3 68 people (34 couples) 4 Carol Roble. 5 François Fernández.

12A It's a world record

1a b4 c8 d6 e5 f2 g9 h7 i1

b b 15,940 c 7,400,000 d 3.14 e 750,000 f 600,000,000 g 0.75 h 86,912

2 2 nicest 3 slimmest 4 most expensive 5 best 6 most boring 7 worst 8 most crowded 9 dirtiest 10 oldest 11 most interesting 12 happiest

3 2 shortest 3 The longest 4 highest 5 the most dangerous 6 most common 7 most expensive 8 the cheapest 9 the biggest

4 2 older 3 richer 4 most intelligent 5 most interesting 6 tallest 7 shorter 8 younger 9 better 10 best 11 worst 12 nearest 13 most important

12B Have you ever ... ?

1a c work d meet e study f have g stay h write v visit j see

b 2 work; worked; worked 3 study; studied; studied 4 stay; stayed; stayed 5 visit; visited; visited 6 go, went; been/gone 7 meet; met; met 8 have; had; had 9 write; wrote; written 10 see; saw; seen

2a 2 have lived 3 've seen 4 's written 5 've stayed 6 have studied 7 's worked

b 2 Tom and Janet haven't lived in the USA. 3 You haven't seen this film before. 4 Federico hasn't written a book. 5 We haven't stayed in the Ritz Hotel. 6 Lee and Wendy haven't studied Portuguese. 7 She hasn't worked for a French company.

3a 2 Has your sister ever studied Italian? 3 Have your children ever seen *Avatar*? 4 Has your son ever played basketball? 5 Have you ever met someone from South Africa? 6 Has it ever snowed on your birthday? 7 Have you ever been to Scotland? 8 Has your mother ever cooked for 20 people? 9 Have you ever worked in a hotel?

b 2 No, she hasn't. 3 Yes, they have. 4 Yes, he has. 5 No, I/we haven't. 6 No, it hasn't. 7 Yes, I/we have. 8 No, she hasn't. 9 No, I/we haven't.

4 2 was 3 worked 4 did ... work 5 Have ... been 6 travelled 7 Did ... enjoy 8 had 9 Have ... visited 10 've been

12C See you soon!

1 2 passport; ticket 3 check-in desk; bag drop 4 hand luggage 5 window; middle; aisle 6 boarding pass 7 flight number; gate 8 on time; delayed 9 passengers

2 2 How many bags 3 pack your bags 4 have you got 5 You're in seat 6 Is that 7 Which gate 8 Is the flight 9 Enjoy your

3 2 boarding pass 3 have 4 have 5 will 6 Don't 7 to send 8 in 9 see 10 don't 11 to send 12 Have 13 Don't

Reading and Writing Portfolio 1

1 2 first name 3 surname 4 house number 5 street name 6 town/city 7 postcode 8 country

3 1 Mr E Stevens
71 Portland St
Manchester
M23 7RX

2 Ms Jane Fox
56 Gilmour Rd
Cambridge
CB1 5NS
UK

4 Hello, my name's Lisa Sanders. I'm British and I'm from **Bristol**, in England. I'm a teacher and I'm married. My address is 67 Wood Rd, **Bristol, BR2 5GL.** My home phone number is 0117 496 3429. I'm in London for a conference this week.

5 2 Lisa 3 Sanders 4 British 5 67 Wood Rd, Bristol 6 BR2 5GL 7 0117 496 3429

Reading and Writing Portfolio 2

1a Kathy B Danny C Sabrina A

b 2 No, it isn't. 3 About three years old. 4 Two. 5 No, it isn't. 6 Yes, it has.

3 2 My brother has got a new car. I think it's a **BMW**. 3 I've got a **Panasonic TV** and a **Sony DVD** player. 4 **Juan's** from **Spain** and his wife's from the **USA**. 5 My address is 13 **Richmond Road, Melbourne, Australia**. 6 We haven't got a **German** car. Our car's **Japanese**.

5 2 Have you got Susan's address? 3 Rob hasn't got any brothers or sisters. 4 Sarah's got a bicycle. It's 50 years old! 5 I've got Jenny's car but I haven't got the keys. 6 My sister's got a camera, a mobile, a DVD player and a new TV. 7 My mother's house isn't very big.

6 I think it's beautiful. It's very fast and it's also very easy to use. I've got all my music, games, films and school work on it. My laptop's very important to me and I love it!

Reading and Writing Portfolio 3

1 3 law student 4 23 years old 5 Wednesdays and Fridays 6 single 8 read a lot, visit friends, go to the cinema

3 2 I don't have breakfast, but I have a big lunch. 3 I get up early in the week because I start work at 6.30 a.m. 4 We don't go to the cinema, but we watch a lot of TV. 5 I want to learn English because I need it for my job. 6 They finish work at 5 p.m. and they get home at 6 p.m. 7 We don't go out a lot because we have three children. 8 I don't live with my parents, but I phone them every day.

4a 10 Curitiba, Brazil 11 history and music teacher 12 31 years old 13 Saturday mornings 14 married 15 Julia (wife), Luciana and Adriano (children) 16 watch TV, visit friends, go to concerts

b 2 and 3 and 4 but 5 and 6 and 7 because 8 and 9 but

Reading and Writing Portfolio 4

1a 2 Italian 3 jazz 4 6.30–11p.m. every day 5 English 6 no music 7 6 p.m.–2 a.m. seven days a week 8 American 9 rock

b 2 08081 570848 3 No, it isn't. 4 Yes, it does. 5 34 6 10 p.m. 7 2 Elm St, Bristol, BS22 2RG

2 Teresa B Robbie C Sarah A
3 2D 3A 4C
4a 2 Shall 3 ideas 4 I'd 5 about 6 sounds 7 Where 8 Let's 9 there
5 3 Have you got 4 what about 5 sounds good. 6 Where shall 7 Let's meet 8 See you

Reading and Writing Portfolio 5

1 2E 3A 4B 5C
2 3 ✓ 4 ✓ 5 ✗ The Japanese restaurant was quite crowded. 6 ✓ 7 ✗ Keira was really friendly. 8 ✗ When Miyu got home she emailed her friends.
3 a4 b2 d3 e5
4a 1 After our classes finished we went for coffee in Leicester Square. 2 When the play ended we went for a meal in a Japanese restaurant. 3 We talked for five minutes and then my friends took some photos.
b at different times
5 2 Martin had dinner and then he watched TV. 3 When I got home I phoned my brother. 4 After I finished the report I went to bed. 5 Gwyneth did her homework and then she went out. 6 After Rowan finished university he went to the USA. 7 When I left university I travelled for six months.

Reading and Writing Portfolio 6

1a 1 The Dance Factory 2 £25 3 a film 4 When I Was Young 5 a concert 6 Brixton Apollo 7 £27.50 8 Just Another Weekend 9 Royal Court Theatre, Haymarket
b 2 By credit card on the phone or from their website. 3 Jazz-rock. 4 Nine hours/9 p.m.–6 a.m. 5 Daniel Palmer, Miranda Ross and Gregory Coleman. 6 A comedy.
2 A5 C7 D3 E2 F6 G4 Christina and Roland want to go to the cinema.
4a No, they didn't, because they went to different cinemas.
b 1 Hi Christina. Where are you? 2 On the bus. Call you when I get there? 3 OK. Want me to get tickets? 4 Yes. Thanks. Bye. 5 Hi Roland. I'm here. Got the tickets? 6 Yes. Where are you? Starts in 5 mins! 7 At Filmworld in Camden. Where are you?

Reading and Writing Portfolio 7

1 2 three 3 A 4 D 5 €1,000 per month 6 A and D 7 A 8 B and C
2 1D 2A 3C
3 2 BH8 6YP 3 Five. 4 Yes, it does. 5 It's a café. 6 No, there isn't. 7 Yes, there is. 8 At the station.
4a 2E 3A 4B 5D
b b3 c2 d4

Reading and Writing Portfolio 8

1 2 Yes, you do. 3 Four months. 4 A department store. 5 No, you don't. 6 Thompson and Noble. 7 No, they don't. 8 37. 9 www.willowbournemouth.com
2 Wayne Moody C Beth Chambers B Fergus Jackson A
3 2T 3F 4F 5T 6T 7F
4b 2E 3D 4B 5C

Reading and Writing Portfolio 9

1b the Black Mountains 3 Snowdon 2 Llandudno 1 Tenby 4
2 2T 3F 4T 5F 6T 7F 8T
3 1D 2A 3C 4E 5B
4 2 Aspen is a popular place to ski in **the** Rocky Mountains in **the** USA. 3 Mount Kilimanjaro is in **the** north of Tanzania in Africa. 4 Bournemouth is a seaside town on **the** south coast of England. 5 Lake Balaton is about 100 km from Budapest, **the** capital city of Hungary. 6 Mar del Plata is a seaside town on **the** east coast of Argentina in South America. 7 Manaus is a city on **the** River Amazon in **the** north of Brazil.

Reading and Writing Portfolio 10

1 2 at home 3 can't 4 doing 5 Samantha's 6 a woman he works with 7 together 8 didn't tell 9 daughter 10 has 11 doesn't like 12 always
2a 2 you 3 it 4 we 5 they 6 me 7 her 8 them 9 my 10 our
b Subject pronouns come **before** verbs. Object pronouns come **after** verbs. Possessive adjectives come **before** nouns.

3 2 Olivia 3 Samantha 4 Jodie 5 Adam 6 Adam and Jodie 7 Adam 8 Samantha 9 Adam and Jodie 10 Angela
4 2 it 3 their 4 she 5 him 6 her 7 they 8 them 9 he 10 her 11 his 12 her 13 her
5 2 their 3 you 4 your 5 him 6 you 7 he 8 his 9 Your 10 her 11 their 12 his 13 your 14 he 15 his

Reading and Writing Portfolio 11

1a 2F 3D 4C 5B 6A
b 2 Brighton Pier. 3 No, you don't. 4 Yes, you can. 5 £30.80 – a family ticket and a child's ticket 6 The Lanes
2 Alejandro went to The Lanes and Brighton Pier.
3c **It's** a very good school and the people **are** very friendly ... I like **my classes very much. My teacher's name is** Caroline. She **was born** in Liverpool ... She's French, she's 29 years old and she's **a** doctor. ... **last** night I went to Brighton Pier. ... Agnès thinks Brighton is boring, but I **don't** agree with her. Would you like to visit me?

Reading and Writing Portfolio 12

1a 2E 3A 4D 5C
b 2 In your suitcase. 3 Yes, you can. 4 Non-EU Passports only. 5 Yes, you can. 6 Yes, you do.
2 1B 2A
3 2T 3T 4F 5F 6T 7F 8F 9T
4 2F 3F 4F 5T 6F 7T
4a 2 spent 3 staying 4 weather 5 lots 6 going 7 See

Holiday activities VOCABULARY 9.1

1 Write these holiday activities.

1 g*o* on h*oliday*
2 h____ a p______
3 g__ d______
4 g__ c_______
5 g__ to m______
6 r___ a c___
7 g__ on a b___ t___
8 s___ in a h____
9 g__ s__________
10 g__ to the b____
11 g__ on a g_____ t___
12 t_____ by p_____ t________

2 Fill in the gaps in Jessica's email with the correct form of the verbs in **1a** and a preposition if necessary.

To: andy.mayhew@onlinemail.com

Hi Andy
Guess what? I'm in Cape Town! I arrived here ten days ago. At the moment I [1] *'m staying in* a very nice hotel in the centre of the city and I [2] *go* sightseeing every day. On my first day here I [3] ________ a guided tour of the city, then I climbed up Table Mountain with two people from the hotel. It was a beautiful evening and we [4] ________ a picnic on the top. And two days ago I [5] ________ a boat trip to Robben Island to see Mandela's cell – you were right, it was really interesting. Yesterday morning I [6] ________ a museum in the centre of Cape Town and then I [7] ________ the beach in the afternoon. Did you know you can [8] ________ diving near Cape Town?
When I'm travelling in the city I always [9] ________ public transport, but last week I [10] ________ a car and drove to a wildlife park about 100 km from Cape Town. One evening we all [11] ________ camping in the bush and some elephants came into our camp in the middle of the night – it was very exciting!!
See you when I get home. Then you can tell me where I can [12] ________ holiday next year!
Lots of love Jessica

Infinitive of purpose GRAMMAR 9.1

3 Make sentences. Use these verbs.

~~get~~	study	buy	visit	stay	have

1 I went to the shops / some bread.
I went to the shops to get some bread.

2 Tourists go to Sydney / the Opera House.

3 A lot of people come to London / English.

4 I went to New York / with an old friend.

5 I went to the butcher's / some meat.

6 We're going to the park / a picnic.

4 Tick the correct sentences. Change the wrong sentences.

1 I'm going out *to* buy some milk.

2 We went to Sydney to see the Opera House. ✓

3 He flew to New York for to see his cousin.

4 We often go to that café for breakfast.

5 I need £100 for buy a camera.

6 Yesterday we went to the park for a picnic.

7 We're going to London to go sightseeing.

8 Gary drove to Brighton to visiting some friends.

9 We went to the market for to buy a carpet.

10 I want to buy some presents for my family.

9B A trip to Egypt

Natural places VOCABULARY 9.2

1 Write the letters in these words.

1 the s *e a*

2 a m _ _ _ _ _ _ _

3 an i _ _ _ _ _

4 the d _ _ _ _ _

5 a f _ _ _ _ _

6 the c _ _ _ _ _ _ _ _ _ _

7 a r _ _ _ _

8 a h _ _ _

9 a l _ _ _

10 a w _ _ _

Comparatives GRAMMAR 9.2

2 Patrick and Juliet are at the airport after their holiday in Egypt. Compare them and write sentences.

1 Patrick is / tall / Juliet.

Patrick is taller than Juliet.

2 Juliet looks / young / Patrick.

____

____

3 Patrick is / hot / Juliet.

____

____

4 Patrick's suitcase is / big / Juliet's.

____

____

5 Juliet looks / happy / Patrick.

____

____

6 Patrick had a / bad / time / Juliet.

____

____

7 Juliet had a / good / time / Patrick.

____

____

The Ritz Hotel

London
opened: 1906
number of rooms: 133
price per night: £275–£3,750
facilities: beauty and fitness room, casino, conference room, 24-hour room service
airport: Heathrow 29 km
number of restaurants and bars: 2
dinner: 5.30–10.00 p.m.
don't miss: traditional English afternoon tea at 11.30, 1.30, 3.30, 5.30 and 7.30.

Raffles Hotel

Singapore
opened: 1887
number of rooms: 103
price per night: £240–£1,950
facilities: 24-hour gym and swimming pool, more than 50 shops, business centre
airport: Changi 25 km
number of restaurants and bars: 15
dinner: 7.00 p.m.–10.00 p.m. in the Tiffin Room
don't miss: the story of the hotel in the Raffles Museum

3 Read about two famous hotels. Then fill in the gaps with the comparative form of the adjectives and *The Ritz* or *Raffles*. Use *than* if necessary.

1 *Raffles* is *older than* (old) *The Ritz* .

2 __________ is ______________ (big) __________ .

3 __________ is ______________ (small).

4 Rooms at __________ are ______________ (cheap) rooms at __________ .

5 __________ is ______________ (expensive).

6 __________ is ______________ (near) to the airport.

7 It's ______________ (easy) to decide where to eat at __________ .

8 It's ______________ (difficult) to decide where to eat at __________ .

9 You can have dinner ______________ (early) at __________ .

10 I think __________ looks ______________ (beautiful) than __________ .

A day out

A Stratford-upon-Avon

B Bath

C Bournemouth

Reading

1 **a** Read about three places where English people often go for a day out. Match descriptions 1–3 to photos A–C.

1 ___ This famous old tourist town has 11 km of beautiful beaches. It's the perfect place to go swimming or go on boat trips. There are lots of lovely parks and gardens to visit and it's a great place to eat out. You can also go to a classical concert or go dancing in one of the excellent nightclubs.

2 ___ This was William Shakespeare's home town. You can visit the houses where he lived or see his plays at one of the Royal Shakespeare Company's three theatres. There are some interesting museums and beautiful 500-year-old houses. You can also go on boat trips and visit traditional English villages.

3 ___ Most people come here to visit the Roman Baths, which are about 2,000 years old. You can see them at the Roman Baths Museum – or have a bath yourself at the Thermae Bath Spa in the city centre. This city is also famous for its beautiful 18th century buildings, and it was the home of the writer Jane Austen. You can learn about her life at the Jane Austen Centre near Queen's Square.

b Read the texts again. Where can you do these things? Write two places if possible.

1 visit museums *Bath and Stratford*
2 go to a beach ____________
3 learn about famous writers ____________
4 go on boat trips ____________
5 go to a classical concert ____________
6 see beautiful old buildings ____________
7 see a play ____________

Deciding what to do REAL WORLD 9.1

2 **a** Una, Rick and Kay live in London. They want to go away for the weekend. Read their conversation. Where do they decide to go? ____________

UNA What do you want [1]*do/to do* at the weekend?
RICK I'd like [2]*go/to go* away somewhere.
KAY Yes, me too. Let's [3]*go/to go* to Stratford. We can [4]*see/to see* a Shakespeare play!
RICK Sorry, but I don't really like Shakespeare. I'd rather [5]*go/to go* to the beach.
UNA Well, would you like [6]*go/to go* to Bournemouth?
RICK Yes, good idea. We can just [7]*sit/to sit* on the beach and relax.
KAY But I went there last month. I'd rather [8]*go/to go* somewhere different.
UNA Well, do you want [9]*go/to go* to Bath? There are lots of nice shops and we can [10]*visit/to visit* the Roman Baths.
RICK OK, let's [11]*do/to do* that. My cousin lives in Bath. Maybe we can [12]*stay/to stay* with him.
KAY Bath it is, then. Do you want [13]*drive/to drive*, or shall we [14]*take/to take* the train?
UNA Let's [15]*go/to go* by train. It's a lot quicker.

b Read the conversation again. Choose the correct verb forms 1–15.

Animals VOCABULARY 9.3

3 Find 12 animals (→↓).

Q	R	A	B	B	I	T	A	V	U	G
M	O	U	Z	K	L	I	O	N	S	O
O	Y	L	B	S	T	G	S	M	H	R
N	C	H	I	C	K	E	N	O	E	I
K	O	G	R	E	A	R	A	U	E	L
E	W	B	D	R	W	I	K	S	P	L
Y	W	O	L	F	O	M	E	E	B	A

Time for a change

Verb patterns (*like doing*, *would like to do*, etc.) VOCABULARY 9.4

1 Put the verbs in the correct form, infinitive with *to* or verb+*ing*.

1 I love *working* here. (work)
2 I really hate ______ for exams. (revise)
3 Do we need ______ some food? (buy)
4 Would you like ______ to the cinema? (go)
5 Do you like ______ sport on TV? (watch)
6 My brother wants ______ to Brazil. (go)
7 I really enjoy ______ in bed at the weekend. (stay)
8 We'd love ______ you next week. (visit)
9 They decided ______ the contract. (sign)
10 I want to stop ______. (smoke)

Reading

2 **a** Read the magazine article. Are these sentences true (T) or false (F)?

1 [F] Georgina's husband retired three years ago.
2 [ ] Georgina and Don didn't like England in the winter.
3 [ ] Georgina doesn't like studying Spanish.
4 [ ] Neil and Violet spoke French before they moved to France.
5 [ ] They don't want to live in England again.
6 [ ] Neil wrote a book about their experiences.

b Read the article again. Choose the correct verb forms 1–17.

Home from home!

Every year thousands of British people sell their homes and move to a place in the sun. But is the grass really greener if you move abroad? We ask two couples how they feel about living in a different country.

Georgina Wilkes

We decided [1]*to come/coming* to Spain two years ago, after my husband, Don, stopped [2]*working/to work*. We live in a place called Nerja, on the Mediterranean coast. We chose Spain because we hated [3]*being/to be* in England in the winter and we wanted [4]*living/to live* somewhere warm. We really love [5]*living/to live* here – the weather is wonderful and the local people are really friendly. Some British people here think they don't need [6]*learning/to learn* Spanish, but I think that's wrong. When you're living in another country, it's important to learn the language. I really enjoy [7]*studying/to study* Spanish and I'd like [8]*becoming/to become* fluent. Then I'd really feel part of Spain.

Neil Garner

My wife, Violet, and I decided [9]*moving/to move* to France about six years ago, and we live in a small village near Bordeaux. When we arrived we were the only British people in the village, so we needed [10]*learning/to learn* French very quickly! At first Violet didn't like [11]*living/to live* here, but now we're part of the village and we don't want [12]*going/to go* back to England. It's so quiet and peaceful here. I enjoy [13]*writing/to write* and I'd love [14]*writing/to write* a book about life in the village. We love [15]*having/to have* people to stay and they all say they'd love [16]*living/to live* here too. We'd like [17]*staying/to stay* here for the rest of our lives.

Reading and Writing Portfolio 9 p80

Stay fit and healthy

Language Summary 10, Student's Book p149

Verb phrases VOCABULARY 10.1

1 Read about how Rita and Keith stay fit and healthy. Choose the correct verbs.

RITA I read an article in the paper about [1]*getting/taking* fit for free, and I think it's a very good idea. Now when I'm in town I don't [2]*do/take* escalators, I walk up the stairs instead. I also [3]*get/do* the housework more quickly than before, which uses extra calories, and I [4]*wash/take* the windows every week. And I go to local shops, not the supermarket, and [5]*spend/carry* the shopping home. And I usually [6]*have/do* a shower not a bath, because that uses more calories too. I also [7]*get on/spend* a lot of time with my grandson – that uses hundreds of calories!

KEITH I'm a lawyer for a big American company and I always [8]*have/get* very stressed at work. In the past I [9]*spent/did* a lot of money on gym membership, but I never had time to go. Now I want to [10]*get/have* fit in my day-to-day life. Every morning I [11]*get on/get off* the bus two stops earlier and then walk to the office. And when I get there I don't [12]*take/carry* the lift, I walk up the stairs instead. I don't drive to the carwash any more, I [13]*spend/wash* the car myself. And I always [14]*do/spend* some exercise at the weekend, either swimming or running. Now I'm a lot fitter than when I [15]*spent/got* hundreds of pounds a year on the gym!

Frequency expressions VOCABULARY 10.2

2 Write these sentences again with the word in brackets.

1 My brother goes cycling every three or four days. (twice)
My brother goes cycling twice a week.

2 Katrina and Alex play tennis every Thursday. (once)

3 We go to the supermarket four times a month. (every)

4 You should take some aspirin in the morning and the evening. (twice)

5 I have an English class on Monday, Wednesday and Friday. (three)

6 We go to the theatre four times a year. (every)

7 My parents always go on holiday in April, July and December. (three)

3 Correct the mistakes in these sentences.

1 I see my grandparents once *a* month.
2 How often you go clubbing?
3 He goes to the gym every weeks.
4 I go to the doctor twice times a year.
5 How often do he play football?
6 I study Spanish three time a week.
7 She visits every week her parents.
8 I phone my mum one a day.

Imperatives GRAMMAR 10.1

4 Fill in the gaps with these imperatives.

~~Keep~~	Open	Don't walk
break	don't touch	Use

should/shouldn't GRAMMAR 10.2

5 Read these tips on how to learn English quickly. Fill in the gaps with *should* or *shouldn't* and these verbs.

~~arrive~~	go	talk	ask
sleep	do	be	study

1 You *should arrive* at your class on time.
2 You ________ late.
3 You ________ to every class.
4 You ________ at home in the evenings.
5 You ________ your homework.
6 You ________ in your first language in class.
7 You ________ the teacher when you don't understand something.
8 You ________ in class!

10B What's she like?

Appearance VOCABULARY 10.3 Character VOCABULARY 10.4

1 Do the puzzle.

Across →

3 Attractive, usually for men.
5 Similar to *thin*.
8 Marilyn Monroe had ________ hair.
12 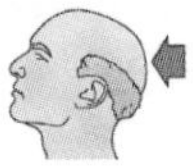
13 A more polite word for *fat*.
15 It's difficult for a ________ person to talk to new people.
16 Old people often have ________ hair.
18 If you're not old or young, you're ________ .

Down ↓

1 She's got  hair.
2 A ________ person makes people laugh a lot.
4 A ________ person likes doing things to help other people.
6 A ________ person doesn't like working.
7  8 
9 An ________ person is friendly and likes talking to new people.
10 Opposite of *tall*.
11 ________ people usually think about themselves and not other people.
14 A ________ person likes giving people money or presents.
17 Opposite of *old*.

Questions with *like* GRAMMAR 10.3

2 **a** Make questions with these words.

1 name / What / his / 's ?

What's his name?

2 he / look / does / What / like ?

______

3 does / like / doing / he / What ?

______

4 like / 's / What / he ?

______

5 you / How / are ?

______

b Read the conversation. Fill in the gaps with the questions from **2a**.

KELLY Hello, Nicky.

a ______

NICKY I'm fine, thanks. I hear you've got a new boyfriend.

b ______

KELLY Well, he's a doctor and he's very good-looking. He's hard-working and reliable, and he's always very generous.

NICKY He sounds very nice.

c ______

KELLY He's tall and he's got blue eyes and blonde hair. Oh, and he's got a little beard.

NICKY d ______

KELLY He likes clubbing, going to the cinema, visiting new places – all the things I like doing.

NICKY e ______

KELLY It's Darren.

NICKY You're joking! My new boyfriend's called Darren and he's a doctor too!

KELLY Really? Oh, dear!

Review: *be* and *have got*

3 **a** Read about these models. Fill in the gaps with *'s got* (= has got), *'ve got* (=have got), *'s* (= is), or *was*.

Natalia Vodianova 1 *was* born in Russia in 1982 and she started modelling when she 2 ______ 15. Natalia moved to Paris when she 3 ______ 17 and soon became a famous model. She 4 ______ 1.76m tall and she 5 ______ light brown hair and blue eyes.
She 6 ______ married to an Englishman, Justin Portman, and they 7 ______ three children.

Lily Cole 8 ______ born in Torquay, in the UK, in 1988. She 9 ______ very tall and she 10 ______ blue eyes. She started modelling when she 11 ______ fourteen years old. She 12 ______ very slim and attractive, and she 13 ______ long red hair. Lily 14 ______ also an actress and she studied History of Art at Cambridge University.

Adriana Lima 15 ______ born in Salvador, Brazil, in 1981. She won the 'Supermodel of Brazil' competition when she 16 ______ only 15. She 17 ______ brown hair and blue eyes, and she 18 ______ 1.78m tall. She 19 ______ married to Marco Jarić, a famous basketball player. They 20 ______ one daughter.

b Read about the models again. Answer these questions.

1 Who was born in Russia? *Natalia*

2 Who's younger, Lily or Natalia? ______

3 Who won a modelling competition? ______

4 Who studied at a famous university? ______

5 Who's taller, Natalia or Adriana? ______

6 Who lived in Paris when she was a teenager? ______

7 Who's married to a famous sports star? ______

I feel ill

Health problems VOCABULARY 10.5

1 Look at the pictures. Write the missing letters.

1

2

3

4
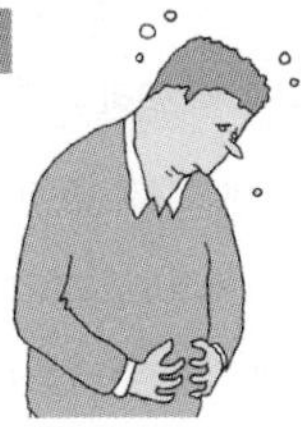
5

6

1 I feel i _l_ _l_ . I think I've got a t _ _ _ _ _ _ _ _ _ _ .
2 I've got a h _ _ _ _ _ _ _ and a s _ _ _ t _ _ _ _ _ .
3 I've got a bad c _ _ _ _ and my b _ _ _ hurts.
4 I've got a s _ _ _ _ _ _ _ a _ _ _ and I feel s _ _ _ .
5 My arm h _ _ _ _ and I've got a t _ _ _ _ _ _ _ _ .
6 I feel t _ _ _ _ _ _ _ . I've got a c _ _ _ .

Treatment VOCABULARY 10.6

2 Fill in the gaps with these words or – (no word). You can use each word more than once.

to the at in off some

go

1 _to_ bed
2 ______ ______ dentist
3 ______ ______ doctor
4 ______ home

stay

5 ______ bed
6 ______ home

take

7 ______ antibiotics
8 ______ day ______
9 ______ cough medicine
10 ______ painkillers

Talking about health REAL WORLD 10.1

3 Read conversations 1 and 2. Then fill in the gaps with these words/phrases.

~~Are you OK~~ You shouldn't I've got feel very well get better soon What's wrong the day off

1
LYN Hi, Bob. [1] _Are you OK_ ?
BOB No, I don't [2] ______________ .
LYN Oh, dear. [3] ______________ ?
BOB I think [4] ______________ a temperature.
LYN Really? [5] ______________ be at work. Take [6] ______________ .
BOB Yes, perhaps I will.
LYN I hope you [7] ______________ .
BOB Thanks a lot, Lyn. See you tomorrow, maybe. Bye.
LYN Bye.

feel sick Get well the matter I feel terrible I've got Are you alright go to the doctor Why don't you

2
IAN Hello, Pat. [8] ______________ ?
PAT No, [9] ______________ .
IAN What's [10] ______________ ?
PAT [11] ______________ a bad stomach ache and I [12] ______________ .
IAN Oh, dear. [13] ______________ go home?
PAT Yes, I think I will.
IAN And I think maybe you should [14] ______________ .
PAT Yes, perhaps.
IAN OK. [15] ______________ soon, Pat.
PAT Thanks a lot. Bye.
IAN Goodbye.

Winter blues

Weather VOCABULARY 10.8

1 Look at the weather around the world. Write sentences about places 1–8.

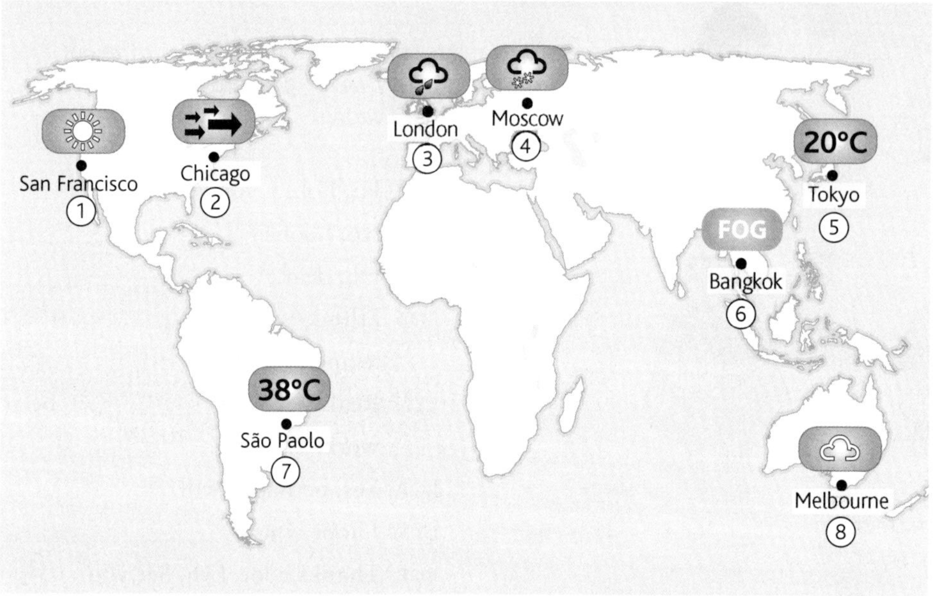

1 It's *sunny in San Francisco.*
2 It's ______
3 ______
4 ______
5 ______
6 ______
7 ______
8 ______

Word building VOCABULARY 10.9 Seasons VOCABULARY 10.7 Reading

2 Read about Manchester and Chicago. Choose the correct words 1–10.

Manchester, in the north of England, is famous for its nightlife, fish and chips, its two football clubs – and, of course, 1*raining/rain*. But does it really 2*rain/raining* more in Manchester than in other British cities? Yes, it does, but in the spring and the summer it's often very 3*sun/sunny*, and sometimes there isn't a 4*cloud/cloudy* in the sky. And in the winter it doesn't always 5*raining/rain* – sometimes it 6*snows/snowing* instead!

Chicago, in the USA, is often called 'the 7*wind/windy* city'. In the winter the 8*wind/windy* is very cold and temperatures in the city are often below zero. There's also lots of 9*snow/snowing* in January and February and it's sometimes very 10*fog/foggy* too. But in the summer it's very hot and the temperature can be 30°C or higher. This is a very good time to enjoy jazz music in the city's parks and clubs, and also to visit its famous museums.

3 **a** Read about the two cities again. Are these sentences true (T) or false (F)?

1 [*T*] Manchester is famous for football.
2 [ ] It rains more in Manchester than in other cities in the UK.
3 [ ] It never snows in winter.
4 [ ] It usually snows at the beginning of the year in Chicago.
5 [ ] It isn't very hot in summer.
6 [ ] You can listen to jazz in Chicago's parks in the summer.

b Find three seasons in the text about Manchester. Which season isn't in the text?

Review: spelling

4 Write the contractions (*I'm*, *don't*, *wasn't*, etc.).

1 ~~She is~~ *She's* married and ~~she has~~ *she's* got two children.
2 We do not like living here because it is too cold.
3 You should not phone when the baby is sleeping.
4 We did not see it because we were not there.
5 They have got three TVs, but two do not work.
6 Matt is sure he was not at the meeting.
7 I would like to move to Spain, but my wife does not want to.

Reading and Writing Portfolio 10 p82

New Year's resolutions VOCABULARY 11.1

1 Which words/phrases do <u>not</u> go with the verbs?

1 **not eat** chocolate *cake/~~smoking~~/sweet things*
2 **lose** *house/weight/three kilos*
3 **get** *fit/a new job/weight*
4 **do more** *exercise/a holiday/a computer course*
5 **have** *fun/a holiday/smoking*
6 **move** *house/a new job/to another country*
7 **work** *hard/fun/less*
8 **stop** *sweet things/working at weekends/smoking*

be going to (1): positive and negative

GRAMMAR 11.1

2 Look at these people's plans for next Saturday. Then fill in the gaps with the correct form of *be going to* and the correct infinitive.

	Andrew	Ingrid	Neil and Mia
meet a friend	✓	✗	✗
clean the house	✗	✓	✓
do some work	✓	✗	✗
go to a party	✓	✓	✓

1 Andrew *is going to meet* a friend.
2 He ______ the house.
3 He ______ some work.
4 Ingrid ______ a friend.
5 She ______ the house.
6 She ______ any work.
7 Neil and Mia ______ a friend.
8 They ______ the house.
9 They ______ any work.
10 All four people ______ to a party.

3 We often use *be going to* when we can 'see' the future in the present. Write sentences for pictures 1–6. Use these phrases.

~~do the washing up~~ have a baby rain clean the car get a taxi play tennis

1

2

3

4

5

6

1 She*'s going to do the washing up.*
2 He ______
3 She ______
4 They ______
5 He ______
6 It ______

be going to (1): *Wh-* questions GRAMMAR 11.2

4 Read the conversations. Write questions with the correct form of *be going to*.

1 EMMA What / you / do after the course ?

[1] *What are you going to do after the course?*

BRUNO I'm going to move to England.

EMMA Really? What / you / do there ?

[2] ______________________

BRUNO I'm going to do a degree in engineering.

EMMA Wow! Where / you / study ?

[3] ______________________

BRUNO At Imperial College, London.

2 CLIVE What / your son / do in the summer ?

[4] ______________________

SHELLEY He's going to travel around Europe.

CLIVE Oh, great! Where / he / stay ?

[5] ______________________

SHELLEY He's going to stay in cheap hotels.

3 MARISA Hi, Ted. Where are you going?

TED To the cinema.

MARISA What / you / see ?

[6] ______________________

TED It's called *Never Again*.

MARISA Oh, right. What / you / do after the film ?

[7] ______________________

TED I don't know.

MARISA Well, would you like to meet for a drink?

TED Yes, that'd be great. Where / you / be ?

[8] ______________________

MARISA At the Sun Café on East Street.

TED OK, I'll see you there at about ten.

MARISA Great. Enjoy the film.

TED Thanks. See you later. Bye.

MARISA Bye, Ted.

11B No more exams!

Studying VOCABULARY 11.2

1 Fill in the gaps with the correct form of these verbs.

~~start~~ pass revise get take

I [1] *started* **college** nearly three years ago and I really enjoy it. I want to be a hotel manager and I need [2] __________ **some qualifications** before I look for a job. It's hard work, of course, and I'm going to [3] __________ my final **exams** at the end of this year. Luckily I [4] __________ all my **exams** at the end of last year and now I [5] __________ for this year's **exams**.

fail go do leave get (x2)

I had a fantastic time at university, but I didn't do much work in my first year and I [6] __________ my **exams**. After that I worked very hard and when I [7] __________ my final **exams** I passed them all. I [8] __________ **a degree** in law and I [9] __________ **a good job** when I [10] __________ university. I think everyone should [11] __________ **to university** if they can.

be going to or *might* GRAMMAR 11.3

2 Read these emails from Austin and Carla. Fill in the gaps with *might* or the correct form of *be going to*.

To: carla.lewis@speedmail.net

Hi Carla
How are you? I'm very happy because I passed my driving test today! I 1 *'m going to* celebrate this evening, but I'm not sure what to do. I 2 *might* go out for a meal or I 3 ______ meet some friends in a bar. One thing's certain – I want to have fun this evening, so I 4 ______ not ______ drive! Do you want to come?
Austin

To: ajroberts@onlinemail.com

Dear Austin
I'm sorry, but I can't come out tonight because I 5 ______ see my sister. But I hope you have a good time. What 6 ______ you ______ do this weekend? I haven't got any definite plans, but I 7 ______ go to that jazz concert in the park. Maybe we could go together?
Love
Carla
PS Congratulations on passing your driving test!

To: carla.lewis@speedmail.net

Hi Carla
I'm sorry, I'm busy this weekend. My brother and I 8 ______ drive to Wales and go climbing. We're not sure where we're going to stay. We 9 ______ camp, or we 10 ______ stay in a hotel – it depends on the weather. Let's meet next week for a drink instead.
Austin

be going to (2): *yes/no* questions and short answers GRAMMAR 11.4

3 **a** Make questions with these words.

1 his driving test / Austin / Is / take / going to ?
Is Austin going to take his driving test?

2 in a bar / meet / going to / Is / some friends / he ?
______

3 Is / this evening / meet / Carla / he / going to ?
______

4 a concert / going to / this weekend / Carla / Is ?
______

5 to Wales / drive / going to / Are / this weekend / Austin and his brother ?
______

6 stay / they / a hotel / Are / in / going to ?
______

b Write the correct answers to the questions in **3a**.

1 *No, he isn't.*
2 *He might.*
3 ______
4 ______
5 ______
6 ______

Review: *be going to* and *might*

4 Correct these sentences.

1 Ed's going to *do* a computer course soon.
2 We might to come and visit you this evening.
3 We're going have dinner on Sunday.
4 Amanda going to move to Australia next year.
5 Tim mights go to the theatre this evening.
6 Sid and Clare going to study in the USA.
7 My brother might studying engineering.

Directions REAL WORLD 11.1

Asking for and giving directions REAL WORLD 11.2

1 **a** Look at the map. Penny is at the station. Read the conversations and choose the correct words.

PENNY Excuse me, where's [1]*a*/*the* hospital?
MAN It's [2]*at*/*on* Morgan Road. [3]*Go*/*Goes* along this road and go [4]*along*/*past* the petrol station. The hospital is [5]*in*/*on* your right.
PENNY Thanks a lot. Bye.

PENNY Excuse me. [6]*Do*/*Are* you know the Cordelia Hotel?
MAN Yes, go along this road and [7]*turn*/*take* right. That's Gunn Street. Go [8]*along*/*over* the bridge and turn right again. The Cordelia Hotel is [9]*in*/*on* your right, opposite the police station.
PENNY Thanks very much.

PENNY Excuse me. [10]*Is*/*Are* there a café [11]*near*/*next to* here?
WOMAN Yes, there's a good one [12]*to*/*in* Angel Street.
PENNY Where's that?
WOMAN Go [13]*along*/*past* this road and turn right. Then turn left before the bridge. There's a café [14]*in*/*on* your left, next to a supermarket. You [15]*can't*/*don't* miss it.
PENNY Thank you. Goodbye.

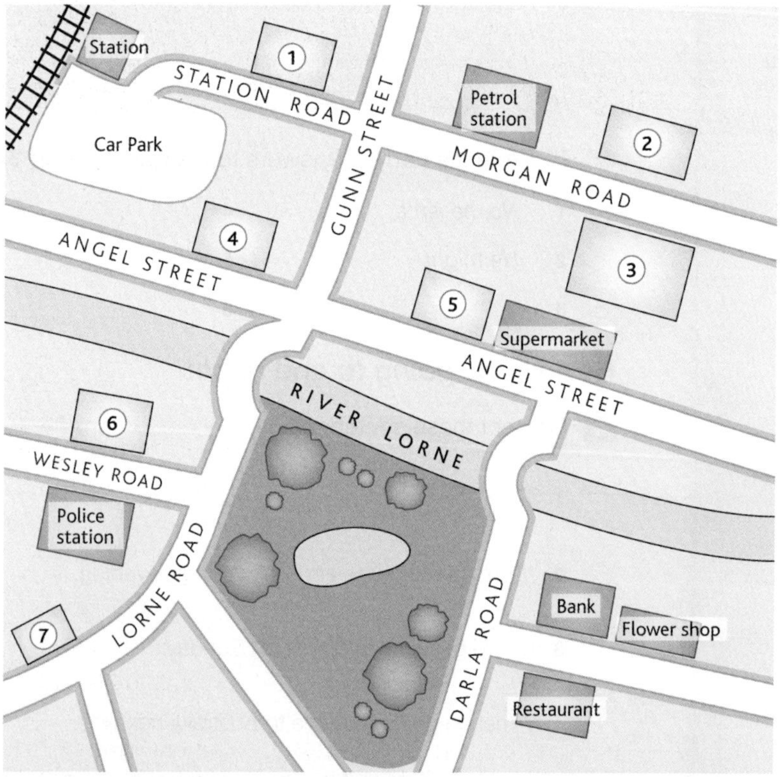

b Read the conversations again. Find these places on the map.

1 The hospital is number ______ .
2 The Cordelia Hotel is number ______ .
3 The café is number ______ .

2 Read these emails and find the places in bold on the map. Then fill in the gaps with the correct words.

To: s.carr@tmail.com

Hi Stephen
Here are directions from **the station** to **the flower shop** where I work. [1] *Go along* Station Road and [2] ______ ______ . That's Gunn Street. Then turn left, [3] ______ ______ a café and turn right [4] ______ a supermarket. [5] ______ ______ the bridge and turn left again. The flower shop is on your left, [6] ______ ______ the bank.
See you tomorrow!
Love Susannah

To: a.bourne@gomail.net

Dear Alice
Here's how to get from **the Cordelia Hotel** to **the restaurant.** Go along Wesley Road and [7] ______ ______ . Then [8] ______ ______ the bridge and turn right. Go [9] ______ a café and turn right again – that's Darla Road. The park is now on your right. [10] ______ ______ after about 100 metres and the restaurant is [11] ______ ______ right, [12] ______ the bank.
See you there at one o'clock.
Charlie

An invitation

Collocations VOCABULARY 11.3

1 Choose the correct verbs.

1 *(stay)/get/rent* with my aunt
2 *rent/stay/book* a flight
3 *get/book/rent* to your place
4 *book/stay/rent* a seat on a train
5 *rent/get/book* married
6 *rent/book/stay* in a hotel
7 *book/stay/rent* a flat
8 *get/book/rent* home
9 *rent/stay/get* at home
10 *stay/book/rent* a train ticket
11 *rent/get/book* divorced
12 *book/stay/rent* a hotel room

Review: collocations

2 Complete the table with these words/phrases.

~~a picnic~~ ~~an exam~~ ~~the cinema~~ ~~running~~ your homework a great time the gym swimming the beach the housework sightseeing a bad cold the washing the doctor clubbing a bath cycling some exercise the dentist a shower

have	**do**
a picnic	*an exam*
go	**go to**
running	*the cinema*

Reading

3 Read the article. Answer these questions.

1 How long was Princess Salama's wedding party?
Seven days.
2 Do more people get married in Las Vegas or the Walt Disney World Resort?

3 How many people got married underwater in Thailand in February 2001?

4 Who got married more often, Linda Lou Essex or Carol Roble?

5 Who was older when they got married, Madeleine Francineau or François Fernández?

Will you marry me?

Lots of people get married, but some people do it a little differently to others. Take a look at these unusual facts about weddings around the world.

- Richard and Carol Roble from New York married each other 56 times, beginning in 1969.
- On 14th February 2001, 34 couples got married underwater off Kradan Island in Thailand.
- About 8,500 people get married every month in Las Vegas in the USA – 'the wedding capital of the world'. Many of these people have an Elvis Wedding, where 'Elvis Presley' sings you a song!
- The marriage of Sheik Rashid Bin Saeed Al Maktoum's son to Princess Salama in Dubai in May 1981 cost $44 million. The party lasted seven days.
- The most married woman in history was Linda Lou Essex from Indiana in the USA, who was married 22 times to 22 different men.
- In June 2000, 120 men in Carandiru Prison in São Paolo, Brazil, married their girlfriends all at the same time. They didn't have a honeymoon!
- More than 2,300 couples get married each year at the Walt Disney World Resort in Florida.
- On 1st February 2002, Madeleine Francineau and François Fernández got married in Clapiers, France. She was 94 years old – and he was 96!

Reading and Writing Portfolio 11 p84

Big and small numbers VOCABULARY 12.1

1 **a** Match the numbers to the words.

a	0.25	1	twenty-five million
b	2.5	2	twenty-five thousand
c	25	3	nought point two five
d	250	4	two point five
e	2,500	5	two thousand, five hundred
f	25,000	6	two hundred and fifty
g	250,000	7	two million, five hundred thousand
h	2,500,000	8	twenty-five
i	25,000,000	9	two hundred and fifty thousand

b Write the numbers.

a three hundred and sixty-five *365*
b fifteen thousand, nine hundred and forty ....
c seven million, four hundred thousand ....
d three point one four ....
e seven hundred and fifty thousand ....
f six hundred million ....
g nought point seven five ....
h eighty-six thousand, nine hundred and twelve ....

Superlatives GRAMMAR 12.1

2 Write the superlatives.

1 cheap *cheapest*
2 nice ....
3 slim ....
4 expensive ....
5 good ....
6 boring ....
7 bad ....
8 crowded ....
9 dirty ....
10 old ....
11 interesting ....
12 happy ....

3 Read the article. Then fill in the gaps in the article with the superlatives of the adjectives in brackets. Use *the* if necessary.

What a strange world!

the Nepalese flag

Nepal has [1] *the most unusual* (unusual) flag in the world. It's the only flag that isn't rectangular.

The world's [2] .... (short) national anthem* is the Japanese national anthem. It's only four lines long.

[3] .... (long) is the Greek national anthem. It's over 600 lines long.

La Paz in Bolivia is the world's [4] .... (high) capital city – it's 3,630 metres above sea level. The Yungas Road, from La Paz across the Andes to Coroico, is [5] .... (dangerous) road in the world.

The world's [6] .... (common) surname is Wang. There are over 92 million people with the surname Wang in China. This isn't very surprising because there are only about 200 Chinese family names.

Tokyo is the world's [7] .... (expensive) city to live in. Johannesburg in South Africa is [8] .... (cheap).

India has [9] .... (big) film industry in the world. It makes over 1,200 films a year.

an Indian cinema

***national anthem = national song**

Review: comparatives and superlatives

4 Read about Joel's family. Choose the correct words.

My name's Joel and I'm the [1]*younger/youngest* person in our family. I've got two sisters and they're both [2]*older/oldest* than me. Erica's an accountant and she's [3]*richer/richest* than both Frances and me. She's also the [4]*more intelligent/most intelligent* person in the family. Frances has got the [5]*more interesting/most interesting* job of us all I think – she's a dancer. But I'm the [6]*taller/tallest* – Frances and Erica are both a lot [7]*shorter/shortest* than me!

My mother's name is Ruby and she's eight years [8]*younger/youngest* than my father, Colin. He's retired now, but he thinks life was [9]*better/best* when he had a job. He enjoys cooking and he's the [10]*better/best* cook in the family. That's good, because my mother is the [11]*worse/worst*! I see my parents more than my sisters because I live the [12]*nearer/nearest*. But the whole family is always together at New Year, which is the [13]*more important/most important* day of the year for us.

12B Have you ever ... ?

Present Perfect: positive and negative

GRAMMAR 12.2

1 **a** Write the verbs.

a viel l*ive*

b og g*o*

c krow w______

d teme m______

e dusty s______

f veha h______

g asyt s______

h treiw w______

i sitvi v______

j ese s______

b Complete these tables with the verbs from **1a**.

REGULAR VERBS

	infinitive	Past Simple	past participle
1	*live*	*lived*	*lived*
2			
3			
4			
5			

IRREGULAR VERBS

	infinitive	Past Simple	past participle
6			
7			
8			
9			
10			

2 **a** Fill in the gaps with the positive form of the Present Perfect. Use contractions (*'ve*, *'s*, etc.) if possible.

1 I*'ve been* to China. (go)

2 Tom and Janet ______ in the USA. (live)

3 You ______ this film before. (see)

4 Federico ______ a book. (write)

5 We ______ in the Ritz Hotel. (stay)

6 Lee and Wendy ______ Portuguese. (study)

7 She ______ for a French company. (work)

b Make the sentences in **2a** negative.

1 *I haven't been to China.*

2 ______

3 ______

4 ______

5 ______

6 ______

7 ______

Have you ever … ? questions and short answers GRAMMAR 12.3

3 **a** Make questions with these words.

1 for / you / Have / a big company / ever / worked ?
Have you ever worked for a big company?

2 studied / ever / your sister / Italian / Has ?

3 ever / *Avatar* / Have / seen / your children ?

4 basketball / ever / Has / your son / played ?

5 Have / met / someone from South Africa / you / ever ?

6 it / on your birthday / snowed / Has / ever ?

7 to Scotland / ever / Have / you / been ?

8 for 20 people / your mother / Has / cooked / ever ?

9 a hotel / you / worked / Have / in / ever ?

b Write short answers for the questions in **3a**.

1 ✓ *Yes, I have.*
2 ✗
3 ✓
4 ✓
5 ✗
6 ✗
7 ✓
8 ✗
9 ✗

4 Ruby works at a travel agent's. She is interviewing Stan for a job. Read the conversation and put the verbs in the correct form of the Present Perfect or Past Simple.

RUBY Hello, Stan. Nice to meet you.
STAN Nice to meet you too.
RUBY Please sit down.
STAN Thank you.
RUBY Right. 1 *Have* you ever *worked* (work) in a travel agent's before?
STAN Yes, I have.
RUBY When 2 ______ (be) that?
STAN Two years ago, before I started university. I 3 ______ (work) for a company called TravelTours in Manchester.
RUBY How long 4 ______ you ______ (work) there for?
STAN For six months.
RUBY 5 ______ you ever ______ (go) to South America?
STAN Yes, I have. Last summer I 6 ______ (travel) around Peru, Chile and Argentina.
RUBY 7 ______ you ______ (enjoy) it?
STAN Yes, I 8 ______ (have) a great time.
RUBY And 9 ______ you ever ______ (visit) any other countries?
STAN Yes, I 10 ______ (go) to India, China, Germany, France, Russia, Poland, Hungary …
RUBY Really! So, when can you start?

See you soon!

Things and places at an airport VOCABULARY 12.2

1 Fill in the missing letters.

1 Before you leave the house, you p *a c k* your b *a g s*.
2 To travel to another country, you need a p _ _ s _ _ _ t and a t _ _ k _ t.
3 When you get to the airport, you go to the c _ _ _ k - i _ d _ _ k or the b _ _ d _ _ p.
4 The person there always asks you if you have any h _ _ d l _ _ g _ _ e.
5 You can choose a w _ _ d _ w seat, a m _ d d _ _ seat or an a _ s _ e seat.
6 The person then gives you your b _ _ _ d _ _ g p _ _ s.
7 You need to listen for your f _ _ g _ t n _ _ b _ r and which g _ _ e your plane leaves from.
8 Usually the plane is o _ t _ _ e, but sometimes it's d _ _ _ y _ d.
9 Then you get on the plane with the other p _ _ s _ _ g _ _ s.

At the airport REAL WORLD 12.1

2 Tom is at the check-in desk. Fill in the gaps in the conversation with these words/phrases.

~~Can I have~~	Which gate	pack your bags
have you got	Is the flight	You're in seat
Enjoy your	How many bags	Is that

MAN Hello. 1 *Can I have* your ticket and your passport, please?
TOM Yes, here you are.
MAN Thank you. 2 ____________ have you got?
TOM Two.
MAN Did you 3 ____________ yourself?
TOM Yes, I did.
MAN And 4 ____________ any hand luggage?
TOM Yes, this bag.
MAN OK. Here's your boarding card. 5 ____________ 23D.
TOM 6 ____________ a window seat?
MAN No, it's an aisle seat.
TOM Oh, OK. 7 ____________ is it?
MAN Gate 19.
TOM 8 ____________ on time?
MAN Yes, it is. Boarding is at 15.30. 9 ____________ flight.

Saying goodbye REAL WORLD 12.2

3 Tom is saying goodbye to his parents. Read their conversation and choose the correct words/phrases.

TOM OK, I've checked in. 1*Boarding/Flight* is at 3.30.
DAD Have you got your 2*everything/boarding pass*?
TOM Yes, I 3*have/I've*, thanks.
DAD Well, 4*have/have got* a nice holiday, Tom.
TOM Thanks, Dad, I 5*have/will*.
MUM 6*Not/Don't* forget 7*send/to send* us an email when you get to your aunt's.
TOM Yes, of course.
DAD Right. See you 8*in/on* two weeks.
TOM Yes, 9*see/seeing* you.
MUM And 10*don't/do* forget 11*to send/sending* your grandmother a postcard.
TOM Yes, of course. Right, I should go …
MUM Oh, Tom?
TOM Yes, Mum?
MUM 12*Have/Do* you got your passport?
TOM Yes, of course! 13*Don't/Not* worry, Mum, I'll be fine. Bye!

Reading and Writing Portfolio 12 p86

At the hotel

Reading addresses; hotel registration forms
Writing capital letters (1); addresses; filling in a hotel registration form
Review *be*; personal details

1 Look at the envelope. Then write these words in the correct places 1–8.

~~title~~ house number town/city postcode
first name street name country surname

1 *title* 5 ______
2 ______ 6 ______
3 ______ 7 ______
4 ______ 8 ______

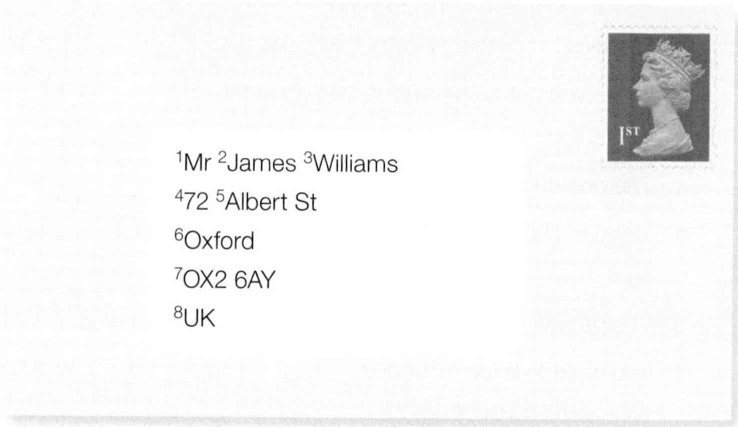

HELP WITH WRITING
Capital letters (1); addresses

2 **a** In English we use capital letters (*A*, *B*, etc.) for these things.

- names: ***R**ebecca **S**mith*
- streets and roads: ***W**alworth **R**d*
- towns and cities: ***L**ondon*
- postcodes: ***SE**6 2**DJ***
- countries: ***UK**, **A**ustralia*
- nationalities: ***B**ritish*

TIP • We say **the** *UK*, but we write *UK* in addresses.

b Notice the short forms we use in addresses. They all start with capital letters.

- *Mr* = a man (married or single)
- *Ms* = a woman (married or single)
- *Mrs* = a married woman
- *Miss* = a single woman
- *Dr* = doctor
- *Rd* = road
- *St* = street

c Underline all the capital letters and short forms on the envelope in **1**.

3 Write these addresses on the envelopes. Use capital letters.

a mr e stevens 71 portland st manchester m23 7rx

b ms jane fox 56 gilmour rd cambridge cb1 5ns uk

1

2

4 Read about Lisa. Then write the capital letters in the correct places.

Hello, my name's ~~l~~ *L* isa sanders. I'm british and I'm from bristol, in england. I'm a teacher and I'm married. My address is 67 wood road, bristol, br2 5gl. My home phone number is 0117 496 3429. I'm in london for a conference this week.

5 Lisa is at the conference hotel. Fill in her hotel form.

Hilder Hotel Park Rd London W1V 9FL
Tel 020 7946 2788 email: enquiries@hilderhotel.co.uk

Registration form

Title	1 *Mrs*
First name	2
Surname	3
Nationality	4
Address	5
Postcode	6
Phone	7
Room number	8 *203*

6 Fill in the form for you.

Hilder Hotel Park Rd London W1V 9FL
Tel 020 7946 2788 email: enquiries@hilderhotel.co.uk

Registration form

Title	
First name	
Surname	
Nationality	
Address	
Postcode	
Phone	
Room number	*412*

7 Read about Lisa in **4** again. Then write five sentences about you.

- Use capital letters.
- Read and check for mistakes.
- Give your sentences to your teacher next class.

Tick the things you can do in English in the Reading and Writing Progress Portfolio, p88.

My favourite thing

Reading people's favourite things
Writing capital letters (2); punctuation; a description of your favourite thing
Review *have got*; personal possessions

1 **a** Read texts 1–3 and match them to photos A–C.

A

B

C

1
KATHY ☐ My favourite thing is my car. It's a Fiat 500 and it's about forty years old. It's red – my favourite colour – and it's got an old radio. It isn't very fast, but I love it. Oh, one more thing – its name is Rose!

2
DANNY ☐ I've got a cat called Jasper. He's about three years old and he's beautiful. He's black and white and he's very friendly. He's got two sisters, Missy and Topsy. Missy is my brother's cat and Topsy is my cousin's cat.

3
SABRINA ☐ What's my favourite thing? It's my new mobile. Of course, it's not just a phone, it's also got all my photos and music on it too. It's a Nokia and it's got an MP3 player, games, videos, the internet, a camera … everything, really!

b Read the texts again. Answer these questions.

1 How old is Kathy's car? *It's forty years old.*
2 Is her car very fast? ____________
3 How old is Danny's cat? ____________
4 How many sisters has Jasper got? ____________
5 Is Sabrina's mobile very old? ____________
6 Has it got all her photos on it? ____________

HELP WITH WRITING
Capital letters (2)

2 **a** When do we use capital letters? Check in **2a** p64.

b We also use capital letters for these things.

- At the beginning of a sentence: ***H**e's about three years old.*
- For the pronoun *I*: *It isn't very fast, but **I** love it.*
- For companies: ***F**iat*, ***N**okia*.
- For some things: *an **MP3** player*, *a **TV**, a **DVD**.*

TIP • We don't use capital letters with nouns: *I've got a car.* not ~~*I've got a Car.*~~

c Look again at the texts in **1a**. Underline all the capital letters.

3 Write these sentences with the correct capital letters.

1 have you got helen's mp3 player?
Have you got Helen's MP3 player?
2 my brother has got a new car. i think it's a bmw.
____
3 i've got a panasonic tv and a sony dvd player.
____
4 juan's from spain and his wife's from the usa.
____
5 my address is 13 richmond road, melbourne, australia.
____
6 we haven't got a german car. our car's japanese.
____

HELP WITH WRITING
Punctuation

4 **a** Notice how we use punctuation.

- We use a full stop (.) at the end of a sentence: *My favourite thing is my car.*
- We use a question mark (?) at the end of a question: *What's my favourite thing?*
- We use an exclamation mark (!) at the end of a surprising sentence: *Its name is Rose!*
- We use commas (,) for lists: *It's got an MP3 player, games, videos, the internet, a camera …*
- We use apostrophes (') for contractions (*'s* = *has*, etc.): *He's got two sisters.*
- We also use apostrophes (') for possessive *'s*: *Topsy is my cousin's cat.*

b Look again at Kathy's text in **1a**. Circle all the punctuation.

5 Write these sentences with the correct punctuation.

1 This isnt my sisters coat

This isn't my sister's coat.

2 Have you got Susans address

3 Rob hasnt got any brothers or sisters

4 Sarahs got a bicycle its 50 years old

5 Ive got Jennys car but I havent got the keys

6 My sisters got a camera a mobile a DVD player and a new TV

7 My mothers house isn't very big

6 Read about Anthony's favourite thing. Then write the text with the correct capital letters and punctuation.

my favourite thing is my laptop i think its beautiful its very fast and its also very easy to use ive got all my music games films and school work on it my laptops very important to me and i love it

My favourite thing is my laptop.

7 **a** Fill in the table about your favourite thing.

What is it?	
how old	
colour	
adjectives (*new*, etc.)	
things it has got	
other information	

b Write about your favourite thing.

- Use the information from the table in **7a**.
- Use capital letters and punctuation.
- Read and check for mistakes.
- Give your description to your teacher next class.

Tick the things you can do in English in the Reading and Writing Progress Portfolio, p88.

All about me

Reading learner profiles
Writing connecting words (1): *and*, *but*, *because*; a learner profile
Review Present Simple

1 The website www.makefriendsinenglish.com is for English learners from around the world. Read about Valentina. Fill in column A in the table.

	A	B	C
name	1 *Valentina Sandri*	9 *Mario Santos*	
town/city and country	2 *Bologna, Italy*	10	
job/study	3	11	
age	4	12	
day(s) of English classes	5	13	
married or single	6	14	
family/relationships	7 *Gianluca (boyfriend)*	15	
free time	8	16	

www.makefriendsinenglish.com

learner profile

Valentina Sandri

Hello, my name's Valentina and I'm 23 years old. I live in Bologna, a beautiful town in the north of Italy. I'm a student at Bologna University. I study law and I'm in my second year. I also study English because I need it for my course. I go to English classes on Wednesdays and Fridays. I'm in Elementary level and I like my classes very much.

I'm not married, but I've got a boyfriend. His name's Gianluca and he's a restaurant manager. I don't see him a lot in the week because the restaurant is open in the evenings, but we always go out on Sundays. In my free time I read a lot and visit friends. I don't watch TV very often, but I go to the cinema every Friday.

I want to write to people who study English and live in a different country to me.

HELP WITH WRITING
Connecting words (1): *and*, *but*, *because*

2 **a** Look at these sentences. Notice how we use *and*, *but* and *because*.

positive	**positive**
I study law.	I'm in my second year.

I study law **and** I'm in my second year.

negative	**positive**
I'm not married.	I've got a boyfriend.

I'm not married, **but** I've got a boyfriend.

what you do	**why you do it**
I study English.	I need it for my course.

I study English **because** I need it for my course.

b Read Valentina's learner profile again. Underline all the examples of *and*, *but* and *because*.

TIP • In sentences with *but*, the negative verb can come first or second: *I don't speak French, but I speak German.* = *I speak German, but I don't speak French.*

3 Write these sentences with *and*, *but* or *because*.

1 I do a lot of sport. I go to the cinema.
I do a lot of sport and I go to the cinema.

2 I don't have breakfast. I have a big lunch.

____

____

3 I get up early in the week. I start work at 6.30 a.m.

____

____

4 We don't go to the cinema. We watch a lot of TV.

____

____

5 I want to learn English. I need it for my job.

____

____

6 They finish work at 5 p.m. They get home at 6 p.m.

____

____

7 We don't go out a lot. We have three children.

____

____

8 I don't live with my parents. I phone them every day.

____

____

4 **a** Read about Mario. Fill in column B in the table in **1**.

www.makefriendsinenglish.com

learner profile

Mario Santos

Hi, my name's Mario. I'm 31 years old [1] *and* live in Curitiba, in Brazil. I'm a teacher [2]__________ I teach history and music. I study English on Saturday mornings [3]__________ I'm in the Elementary class. My classes are great, [4]__________ I don't always do my homework!
I'm married [5]__________ my wife's name is Julia. We've got two children, Luciana and Adriano. Luciana's three [6]__________ Adriano's five. I don't go out in the week [7]__________ I want to be at home with my family. In my free time I watch TV [8]__________ visit friends. I never go to the cinema, [9]__________ I sometimes go to concerts at the weekends. I want to write to an English student in another country.

b Fill in the gaps in Mario's learner profile with *and*, *but* or *because*.

5 **a** Fill in column C in the table in **1** for you.

b Write your learner profile for the website.

- Use the information about you in the table in **1**.
- Use *and*, *but* and *because*.
- Use capital letters and punctuation.
- Read and check for mistakes.
- Give your profile to your teacher next class.

Tick the things you can do in English in the Reading and Writing Progress Portfolio, p88.

Going out

Reading restaurant adverts
Writing messages (1): an email
Review Present Simple; suggestions; requests

1 **a** Read adverts A–C for places to eat in Bristol, England. Then fill in the table.

place	opening times	type of food	type of music
La Trattoria	1 *Tues–Sun 12–11.30 p.m.*	2	3
The Goodwood Hotel	4	5	6
The Boston Bar	7	8	9

b Read the adverts again. Then answer the questions.

1 Is the Italian restaurant open on Mondays?
No, it isn't.

2 What's the phone number of the hotel?

3 Is The Boston Bar open at lunchtime?

4 Does the Italian restaurant have music on Sundays?

5 How many rooms has the hotel got?

6 What time does the music start in The Boston Bar?

7 What's the address of the Italian restaurant?

A

La Trattoria

Traditional Italian Restaurant
pizza, pasta, salads
Open Tues–Sun 12–11.30 p.m.
Live jazz every evening from 8 p.m.
2 Elm St, Bristol, BS22 2RG
Tel: 0117 496 3455

B

THE GOODWOOD HOTEL

67 Goodwood Rd, Bristol, BS13 4RS
Stay in one of our 34 luxury rooms or have dinner in our traditional English restaurant (open 6.30–11 p.m. every day).
WEDDINGS | ANNIVERSARIES | CONFERENCES
For reservations call **08081 570848**
or email us at **enquiries@goodwoodbristol.com**

C

THE BOSTON BAR

Have a drink and relax in our friendly American-style bar.
Try our world-famous burgers!
Open 7 days a week 6 p.m.–2 a.m.
Live rock music every night from 10 p.m.
23 Clifton Rd, Bristol, BS8 6RT Tel: 0117 496 1097
Great food, great music, great people!

2 Teresa, Robbie and Sarah live in Bristol. Read about their plans for the weekend. Choose a restaurant A–C for each person.

TERESA ☐ It's my husband Derek's birthday on Saturday. We want to go to a nice quiet restaurant with our children, Jenny and Liam. Jenny doesn't like Italian food and Liam only eats English food. My husband isn't a problem – he eats anything!

ROBBIE ☐ My friend Ian wants to go out on Saturday evening. He really likes going to places with music, but he hates jazz. And I don't want to go to a restaurant that closes before midnight.

SARAH ☐ I want to go out on Saturday night with my friend Gloria. We'd like to go to a nice restaurant with good food. Gloria loves pizza and I want to go to a place with live music.

3 Robbie and Ian email each other about Saturday night. Put their emails in the correct order.

A ☐
That sounds good. Where shall we meet?
Ian

C ☐
Let's meet at the bar at nine. The address is 23 Clifton Rd. See you there.
R

B *1*
Hi Robbie
What do you want to do on Saturday night? Shall we go to a bar? I'd like to go to a place with music. Have you got any ideas?
Ian

D ☐
Hi Ian
What about The Boston Bar? It's got live music and it closes at 2 in the morning.
Robbie

HELP WITH WRITING
Messages (1): an email

4 **a** Look at the emails in **3** again. Fill in the gaps in these sentences with one word.

MAKING SUGGESTIONS

1 What do you *want* to do?

2 ________ we go to (a bar)?

3 Have you got any ________ ?

4 ________ like to go to (a place with music).

5 What ________ (The Boston Bar)?

6 That ________ good.

PLANNING TO MEET

7 ________ shall we meet?

8 ________ meet at (the bar) at (nine).

9 See you ________ .

b Notice what we say in emails to friends.

- We often begin emails to friends with *Hi + name*.
- We usually end with our first name (*Robbie*) or the initial of our first name (*R*).
- We don't write emails in capital letters. It's not very polite.

5 Complete Sarah and Gloria's emails. Use the phrases in **4a** to help you.

Hi Sarah
How are you? [1] *What do you want to do* on Saturday? [2] *I'd like* to go to a restaurant.
[3] ________________ any ideas?
Gloria

Hi Gloria
Yes, [4] ________________ La Trattoria?
It's in Elm Street. It's an Italian restaurant – and it's got live jazz.
Sarah

Italian food and jazz? Yes, that
[5] ________________ .
[6] ________________ we meet?
G

[7] ________________ at the restaurant.
[8] ________________ there at about eight.
S

6 **a** You want to go out on Saturday night with a friend. Make notes on these things.

- the place you want to go to
- why you want to go there (food, music, etc.)
- time and place to meet

b Write an email conversation between you and your friend. Write four messages.

- Use your notes from **6a**.
- Use phrases from **4a** in your emails.
- Read and check for mistakes.
- Give your emails to your teacher next class.

Tick the things you can do in English in the Reading and Writing Progress Portfolio, p88.

Reading and Writing Portfolio 5

A night to remember

Reading a student's composition
Writing paragraphs (1); connecting words (2): *after*, *when*, *and then*; a composition
Review Past Simple; adjectives

1 Read about Miyu's evening out. Then put the pictures in order.

The day I met Keira ...

1 A few years ago I went to the UK with two friends to study at a language school in London. The day after I arrived was a very special day for me because it was my 21st birthday. After our classes finished we went for coffee in Leicester Square.

2 Then we went to the theatre to see a play called *The Children's Hour*. I wanted to see it because my favourite actress, Keira Knightley, was in it. We sat in a box and had a very good view. The play was really good and Keira Knightley was wonderful.

3 When the play ended we went for a meal in a Japanese restaurant near the theatre. It was quite crowded, but the food was great. We had sushi and salad – it was very nice. After the meal my friends gave me presents and then the whole restaurant sang Happy Birthday!

4 After we left the restaurant we walked past the theatre again – and there was Keira Knightley! I went over and said hello and she was really friendly to me. We talked for about five minutes and then my friends took some photos of me and Keira together.

5 When I got home I emailed all my friends in Japan and told them about my birthday. I also sent them the photos of me and Keira! It really was a night to remember.

2 Read the text again. Tick the true sentences. Correct the false sentences.

1 Miyu went to London with two friends.

✓

2 The day after they arrived was Miyu's 18th birthday.

It was Miyu's 21st birthday.

3 Keira Knightley is her favourite actress.

____

4 Miyu liked *The Children's Hour*.

____

5 The Japanese restaurant was quite empty.

____

6 Miyu met Keira Knightley in the street.

____

7 Keira wasn't very friendly.

____

8 When Miyu got home she phoned her friends.

____

HELP WITH WRITING
Paragraphs (1); connecting words (2): *after, when,* and *then*

3 Match a–e to paragraphs 1–5 in the text.

a ☐ meeting Keira
b ☐ at the theatre
c [1] introduction
d ☐ at the restaurant
e ☐ the end of the evening

TIPS • We usually start a new paragraph when we talk about a different place or time.
• We don't start a new paragraph for every new sentence.

4 **a** Look at these sentences. Notice how we make sentences with *after, when* and *and then*. Underline the verb that happened first.

1 **After** our classes finished we went for coffee in Leicester Square.
2 **When** the play ended we went for a meal in a Japanese restaurant.
3 We talked for about five minutes **and then** my friends took some photos.

b Choose the correct answer in the rule.

- We often use *after, when* and *and then* for things that happen ***at the same time/at different times***.

c Underline all the examples of *after, when* and *and then* in the text.

TIP • We can also use *then* without *and*. We usually use a comma (,) before *then*: *We talked for about five minutes,* ***then*** *my friends took some photos.*

5 Put these sentences together. Use the words/phrases in brackets.

1 I left the party. I went home. (after) *After I left the party I went home.*
2 Martin had dinner. He watched TV. (and then)
3 I got home. I phoned my brother. (when)
4 I finished the report. I went to bed. (after)
5 Gwyneth did her homework. She went out. (and then)
6 Rowan finished university. He went to the USA. (after)
7 I left university. I travelled for six months. (when)

6 **a** Think of a night to remember that you had in the last six months – or invent one! Look at these questions and make notes in the table.

When was it? Where did you go? Who did you go with?	1
What did you do there (food, drink, music, etc.)? What did you like about it?	2
Where did you go after that? Did you have a good time?	3
When did you get home? What did you do when you got home?	4

b Write about your night to remember.

- Use your notes from **6a**.
- Start a new paragraph for information 1–4 in the table.
- Use *when, after* and *and then*.
- Read and check for mistakes.
- Give your composition to your teacher next class.

Tick the things you can do in English in the Reading and Writing Progress Portfolio, p88.

Text me!

Reading entertainment adverts
Writing messages (2): a text message
Review free time activities; suggestions

1 **a** Look at the adverts for things to do in London. Fill in gaps 1–9 in the table.

event	name	place	price
a club night	Happy House Night	1	2 £
3	4	Filmworld Leicester Square Filmworld Camden	
5	Last Laugh	6	7 £
a play	8	9	

b Read the adverts again. Answer these questions.

1 What type of film is *When I Was Young*?

A love story.

2 How do you buy tickets for the Happy House Night?

3 What type of music do Last Laugh play?

4 How long can you dance for at the Dance Factory?

5 Who are the actors in *When I Was Young*?

6 What type of play is *Just Another Weekend*?

2 It's Saturday afternoon. Roland and Christina want to go out in the evening. Put their text messages in order. What do they want to do?

HELP WITH WRITING
Messages (2); a text message

3 **a** Look again at **2**. Notice how we often miss out these types of word in text messages.

- **subject pronouns:**
  ~~I~~ Think it's good. ~~I~~ love you.
- **subject pronouns and auxiliary verbs:**
  ~~Do you~~ Want to go to the cinema tonight?
  ~~I'll~~ See you there.
- **short answers:**
  Yes, ~~I do~~.

b Look at how we use these short words and sentences in text messages. Notice which words we often miss out in sentences 4–7.

1 Hello. → Hi.
2 Goodbye. → Bye.
3 Thank you. → Thanks.
4 ~~That's a~~ Good idea.
5 Which film ~~do you want to see~~?
6 Which cinema ~~shall we go to~~?
7 ~~Shall we~~ Meet at Filmword at 8?

4 **a** Read Roland and Christina's text messages on Saturday evening. Did they see the film? Why?/Why not

b Read messages 1–8 again. Change or cross out the underlined words.

5 **a** Imagine you're in London. It's Saturday afternoon. Look again at the adverts on p74. Make notes on these things.

- What you want to do tonight.
- A friend you want to go with.
- Where you and your friend are now.
- Where and when you want to meet him/her.

b Write a text message conversation between you and your friend. Write four messages.

- Use your notes from **5a**.
- Don't use pronouns or auxiliary verbs at the beginning of sentences.
- Use short sentences and short words.
- Read and check for mistakes.
- Give your messages to your teacher next class.

Tick the things you can do in English in the Reading and Writing Progress Portfolio, p88.

Renting a flat

Reading adverts for places to live
Writing paragraphs (2); a letter to a friend
Review *there is/there are*; places in a town/the country

PLACES TO LET

A

Firhouse
South Dublin City
*House to let**
2 bedrooms, bathroom, new kitchen, large living room. Near park and buses to city centre. Very quiet area. Shopping centre 8 mins. No pets*.
€850 per month

B

Clontarf
North Dublin City
Flat to let
2 bedrooms, bathroom with separate toilet. Large kitchen and living room with view of city. Quiet street. Near station (5 mins) and shops. Non-smokers* only.
€1,000 per month

C

Smithfield
Dublin City Centre
Flat to let
1 bedroom, bathroom, large kitchen and living room with balcony. 10 min walk to city centre. Bus stop 1 min, station 5 mins. Non-smokers only.
€700 per month

D

Castleknock North Dublin
City House to let
1 double bedroom, 2 single bedrooms, 2 bathrooms, large kitchen, 2 living rooms. Small garden. Near Castleknock village, Phoenix Park, shops and restaurants. 10 min walk to station.
€1,450 per month

**to let* = for rent **a pet* = an animal (for example, a cat or a dog) you have in your house **a non-smoker* = a person who doesn't smoke cigarettes

1 Read the adverts for houses and flats in Dublin, Ireland. Then answer these questions.

1 How much is the house in Firhouse? *€850 per month*
2 How many bedrooms are there in the house in Castleknock? ______
3 Which place isn't near a station? ______
4 Which place is near a village? ______
5 How much is the flat in Clontarf? ______
6 Which two places are near a park? ______
7 Which place doesn't want people with pets? ______
8 Which two places don't want smokers? ______

2 Read about these people and choose the best flat/house A–D for them.

1 ☐ Harry and Beth McCaffrey are from Edinburgh, Scotland. They've got two children, a boy and a girl, and a dog. They want to be near a station and a park. Maximum rent per month = €1,500.

2 ☐ Gary and Katy Richardson live in Bournemouth, in England. Katy's got a new job in the centre of Dublin. Gary's a writer and works at home. Gary smokes, but Katy doesn't. Maximum rent per month = €1,000.

3 ☐ Michael O'Brien lives in Dublin and he wants to find a new flat. He lives alone and he's got two cats. He wants to be near the town centre. He's got a car and he doesn't smoke. Maximum rent per month = €850.

3 Richard wants to rent Gary and Katy's flat in Bournemouth. Read Gary's letter to Richard. Then answer questions 1–8.

> **A** 46 Brook St
> Bournemouth
> BH8 6YP
>
> **B** 14th April
>
> **C** Dear Richard,
>
> **1** How are you? Katy and I are fine and life here in Bournemouth is good.
>
> **2** Let me tell you about the flat. There are two bedrooms, a bathroom, a kitchen, a living room and a small garden. There's also a TV and a DVD player in the living room.
>
> **3** The flat's near some shops and there's a great café called The Resting Place at the end of our road. We aren't near a station, but there are lots of buses to the town centre. And it's only a ten-minute walk to the beach!
>
> **4** Phone me when you arrive and we can meet you at the station. See you soon.
>
> **D** Best wishes,
>
> **E** Gary
>
> PS My mobile number is 07700 900326.

1 What is the number of Gary and Katy's house?

46

2 What's Gary and Katy's postcode?

____

3 How many rooms are there in the flat?

____

4 Does the house have a garden?

____

5 What is 'The Resting Place'?

____

6 Is there a station near the flat?

____

7 Is there a beach near the flat?

____

8 Where can Gary and Katy meet Richard?

____

HELP WITH WRITING
Paragraphs (2): a letter to a friend

4 **a** Notice how we write a letter. Match 1–5 with A–E on the letter.

1 [*C*] the beginning of the letter
2 [ ] the person's name
3 [ ] the address
4 [ ] the date
5 [ ] the end of the letter

b Match a–d to paragraphs 1–4 in the letter.

a [*1*] greetings
b [ ] places near the flat
c [ ] the flat
d [ ] planning to meet

c Notice what we say in letters to friends.

- We usually begin with *Dear* + name.
- We end a letter with *Best wishes* or *Love*. We often use a comma after these words/phrases.
- We use *PS* for extra information at the end of the letter.

5 **a** Imagine a friend wants to rent your house or flat. Make notes on what to say in your letter.

PARAGRAPH	
1 greetings	
2 rooms and things in the house or flat	
3 places near the house or flat	
4 planning to meet	

b Write a letter about your house or flat to your friend.

- Use your notes from **5a**.
- Use the information in **4** to help you.
- Read and check for mistakes.
- Give your letter to your teacher next class.

Tick the things you can do in English in the Reading and Writing Progress Portfolio, p88.

Finding a job

Reading job adverts
Writing a formal letter
Review jobs; requests

1 Read these adverts for jobs in the UK. Answer these questions.

1 Who do you email for an application form at Nature Adventures Ltd?
Dave Jones.

2 Do you need experience to be a receptionist at the Willow Hotel?
______

3 How long is the contract for summer camp group leaders?
______

4 What type of shop is Thompson and Noble?
______

5 Do you need experience to be a summer camp group leader?
______

6 Which company does Fran James work for?
______

7 Do receptionists at the Willow Hotel always work from Monday to Friday?
______

8 How many hours do sales managers at Thompson and Noble work a week?
______

9 What is the website of the Willow Hotel?
______

A

THE WILLOW HOTEL

Receptionist

We are looking for a friendly person to work in reception in our popular tourist hotel. Five days per week, including some evening and weekend work. Some experience* needed.

For an application form* and details of how to apply please go to: www.willowbournemouth.com/jobs

B

SALES MANAGER

Thompson and Noble is a large department store in the centre of Cambridge. We are looking for sales managers to work in our men's and women's clothes department. Some experience needed. 37-hour week, including some weekend work.

For an application form, please go to: www.thompson&noble.co.uk/jobs
Email all application forms to Fran James at f.james@t&n.co.uk

C

GROUP LEADERS WANTED

Nature Adventures Ltd are looking for group leaders to work at our children's summer camps in the UK. Four-month contract: June–Sept.

If you love outdoor sports, have lots of energy and enjoy working with children, we would like to hear from you. No experience needed.

For an application form, email Dave Jones at d.jones@natureadventures.com or download from www.natureadventures.com/forms

**experience* = you did the same job in the past
**an application form* = a form you fill in to get a job

2 Read about these people. Match them to the job adverts A–C.

name	**Wayne Moody** ☐	**Beth Chambers** ☐	**Fergus Jackson** ☐
address	47 Market St Brighton BN4 3SG	54 Robins St Newmarket CB8 3WS	34 Hill St Poole BN15 8JH
job	University student. Last year worked at The Highland Outdoor Centre in Scotland for three months.	Manager at One Stop, a clothes shop in Newmarket. Started two years ago.	Receptionist at Sea View Hotel, Poole. Started six months ago.
other information	Likes working with children, enjoys horse riding and windsurfing.	Loves fashion and women's clothes, can work weekends.	Loves working with tourists, can work evenings and weekends.

47 Market St
A Brighton
BN4 3SG

B 22nd April

C Mr D Jones
Nature Adventures Ltd
Dartmoor
Devon
EX22 6KH

Dear Mr Jones

I would like to apply for the job of summer camp group leader.

I am a student in my second year at university and I am looking for work for the summer. Last year I worked at The Highland Outdoor Centre in Scotland for three months. I like working with children and I enjoy all sports, particularly horse riding and windsurfing.

Could you please send me an application form and any other information about your company?

I look forward to hearing from you.

Yours sincerely

D W Moody

E Wayne Moody

3 Read the letter. Are these sentences true or false?

1 [T] Wayne Moody wrote the letter.
2 [ ] He wants to be a summer camp group leader.
3 [ ] He hasn't got any experience.
4 [ ] He started university three years ago.
5 [ ] He can ride a horse.
6 [ ] He wants an application form.
7 [ ] He wrote the letter in March.

HELP WITH WRITING A formal letter

4 **a** Notice how we write a formal letter. Match 1–5 to A–E on the letter.

1 [A] your address (but not your name)
2 [ ] your full name
3 [ ] your signature
4 [ ] the date
5 [ ] the name and address of the person you are writing to

b Notice how we begin and end a formal letter.

If we **know** the person's name:

- we begin the letter with: *Dear Mr/Mrs/Ms + surname*
- we end the letter with: *Yours sincerely*

If we **don't know** the person's name:

- we begin the letter with: *Dear Sir/Madam*
- we end the letter with: *Yours faithfully*

c Notice what we say in formal letters.

- We don't use contractions: *I would* not ~~*I'd*~~, *I am* not ~~*I'm*~~
- We use polite phrases: *I would like* not ~~*I want*~~ *Could you please … ?* not ~~*Can you … ?*~~
- We often end the letter with: *I look forward to hearing from you.*

d Underline the phrases in **4c** in the letter.

5 Look again at the information in **2**. Write a letter from Beth or Fergus to one of the companies in the adverts and ask for an application form.

- Use the information in **4** to help you write your letter.
- Remember to use paragraphs.
- Read and check for mistakes.
- Give your letter to your teacher next class.

Tick the things you can do in English in the Reading and Writing Progress Portfolio, p88.

Reading and Writing Portfolio 9

Places to go

Reading tourist information
Writing describing places: paragraphs (3); phrases with and without *the*
Review places in a town; *can*

1 **a** Tick the words you know. Check the other words/phrases in a dictionary.

the coast   a view   scenery   go surfing   an ocean   a castle

b Read this tourist information about Wales. Then match these places to 1–5 on the map.

Cardiff [5]   the Black Mountains [ ]   Snowdon [ ]   Llandudno [ ]   Tenby [ ]

http://www.placestogo.com

EUROPE » THE UK » WALES

www.placestoGO.com

Facts about the country

A Wales is part of the United Kingdom and it's famous for its beautiful scenery, music festivals and friendly people. It has its own language, Welsh, but nearly everyone speaks English. Wales is also famous for its long place names – like Llanfairpwllgwyngyllgogerychwyrndrobwllllantysiliogogogoch! The best time to visit is from June to September.

Places to visit and things to do

B Cardiff is the capital city of Wales. It's a busy, modern city on a river called the Taff. There's a beautiful castle in the centre of the city and some interesting museums. St David's Hall is a good place for traditional Welsh music. You can also go to concerts and sports events at the amazing Millennium Stadium.

C Brecon Beacons National Park is a great place for walks and picnics. You can walk along Offa's Dyke in the Black Mountains and enjoy the wonderful views, or go fishing at Llangorse Lake, the largest natural lake in south Wales.

D Snowdonia National Park is in the north of the country. Every year about 500,000 people climb Snowdon, the highest mountain in Wales. You can also travel up the mountain by train!

E Llandudno is an old seaside town on the north coast. It's famous for its long beaches and beautiful scenery, and it's a good place to go surfing. You can also go surfing at many places in the south of the country, like Broadhaven and Tenby.

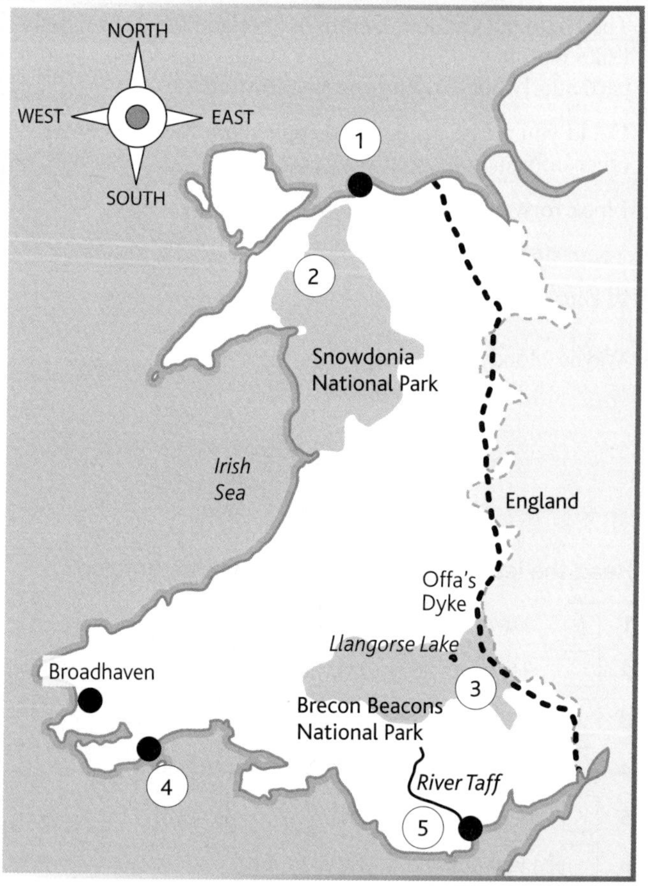

2 Read the information again. Are these sentences true (T) or false (F)?

1 [T] Wales is a country in the UK.
2 [ ] They speak two languages in Wales.
3 [ ] August isn't a good time to visit.
4 [ ] You can listen to music at the Millennium Stadium.
5 [ ] Snowdon is in the Black Mountains.
6 [ ] You can travel by train up Snowdon.
7 [ ] Llandudno is a modern town.
8 [ ] Wales is a good place for surfing.

HELP WITH WRITING Describing places

Paragraphs (3)

3 **a** Look at the tourist information again. Match 1–5 to paragraphs A–E.

1 ☐ the country's highest mountain
2 ☐ general information about the country
3 ☐ places to go walking
4 ☐ places to go surfing
5 ☐ things to do in the capital city

Phrases with and without *the*

b Look at these useful phrases for describing places. Notice when we use *the* in these phrases.

- *It's famous for its …*
- *The best time to visit is from … to …*
- *… is a good/great place for …*
- *You can (also) …*
- *There's a … in the centre of the city.*
- *… on the north coast*
- *… in the south of the country*
- *… is the capital city*

c Underline the phrases in **3b** in the tourist information on the website.

d Notice when we use *the* and when we don't use an article with these places.

THE

- rivers: *the Taff, the Nile*
- seas and oceans: *the Irish Sea, the Atlantic Ocean*
- some countries: *the UK, the USA*
- mountain ranges: *the Black Mountains, the Himalayas*

NO ARTICLE

- most countries: *Wales, Brazil*
- cities and towns: *Cardiff, Tenby*
- mountains: *Snowdon, Mount Fuji*
- continents: *Europe, Asia*
- lakes: *Llangorse Lake, Lake Geneva*

4 Read these sentences about popular places for tourists. Fill in the gaps with *the* or – (no article).

1 There's a beautiful castle in *the* centre of *–* Edinburgh, in *–* Scotland.
2 Aspen is a popular place to ski in ______ Rocky Mountains in ______ USA.
3 ______ Mount Kilimanjaro is in ______ north of ______ Tanzania in ______ Africa.
4 Bournemouth is a seaside town on ______ south coast of ______ England.
5 ______ Lake Balaton is about 100 km from ______ Budapest, ______ capital city of ______ Hungary.
6 Mar del Plata is a seaside town on ______ east coast of ______ Argentina in ______ South America.
7 Manaus is a city on ______ River Amazon in ______ north of ______ Brazil.

5 **a** Make notes about your country.

facts about the country	places to visit and things to do

b Write a description of your country for the www.placestogo.com website.

- Use your notes from **5a**.
- Use different paragraphs for each place.
- Use phrases from **3** and check for *the*/no article.
- Read and check for mistakes.
- Give your description to your teacher next class.

Tick the things you can do in English in the Reading and Writing Progress Portfolio, p88.

The advice page

Reading letters asking for advice
Writing pronouns and possessive adjectives; a letter of advice
Review *should/shouldn't*; *Why don't you … ?*

1 Read letters A–C. Then choose the correct answers.

1 Jasper broke his leg *in a car accident/doing sport.*
2 He stayed *at home/in hospital* for four months.
3 He *can/can't* cycle very fast.
4 He doesn't like *watching/doing* sport.
5 Adam is *Olivia's/Samantha's* boyfriend.
6 Last night Adam was in a restaurant with *Olivia's sister/a woman he works with.*
7 They left the restaurant *at different times/together.*
8 Olivia *told/didn't tell* her sister about what happened.
9 Maria is Yvonne's *daughter/friend.*
10 Rick *has/hasn't* got a job.
11 He *likes/doesn't like* putting Maria to bed.
12 He *always/sometimes* goes out on Saturday night.

Ask Angela

If you've got problems,
Angela Armstrong is here to help.

A Four months ago **I** was in a car accident and I broke **my** leg very badly. **It**'s OK now, but I'm quite overweight at the moment because I spent four months just sitting at home. My wife says I should lose about ten kilos and I agree with **her**. Last weekend **we** went cycling with **our** friends, but **they** were all faster than **me** and I lost **them**! And I really hate doing sport – it's really boring! I want to lose weight without doing any exercise. Can **you** give me some advice?
Jasper, Northampton

B [1]**I**'ve got a big problem with [2]**my** sister, Samantha. Last night I saw [3]**her** boyfriend, Adam, in a restaurant with another woman. Her name is Jodie and [4]**she** works in [5]**his** office. [6]**They** both looked very happy and [7]**he** left the restaurant with her, arm in arm. I didn't call my sister because I didn't want to hurt [8]**her**. Now I don't know what to do. Should I tell her I saw [9]**them** together, or should I talk to Adam first? What do [10]**you** think I should do?
Olivia, Brighton

HELP WITH WRITING
Pronouns and possessive adjectives

2 **a** Look at the words in bold in letter A. Write them in the table.

subject pronouns	object pronouns	possessive adjectives
1 *I*	6	9
2	you	your
He	him	his
She	7	her
3	it	its
4	us	10
5	8	their

b Look at these sentences. Then complete these rules with before and after.

I broke ***my*** *leg four months ago.*
She saw ***them*** *in a restaurant.*

- Subject pronouns come ______________ verbs.
- Object pronouns come ______________ verbs.
- Possessive adjectives come ______________ nouns.

TIP • Notice the difference between *it's* and *its*.
It's OK now. (*it's = it is*)
What's its name? (*its* = possessive adjective)

3 Read letter B again. Which people do the words in bold 1–10 refer to?

1 *Olivia*
2 ______________
3 ______________
4 ______________
5 ______________
6 ______________
7 ______________
8 ______________
9 ______________
10 ______________

C I'm married and we've got a new baby, Maria. She's our first child and she's only two months old. The problem is that my husband, Rick, never helps me with our daughter. He works very hard, I know, but when he gets home from work he just watches TV and waits for his dinner. When I ask him to put Maria to bed, he always says that he's too tired. But he goes out with his friends every Saturday night – he's never too tired for them! Can you help me?

Yvonne, Manchester

Have you got a problem?
Email me at **askangela@mylife.co.uk**

4 Read Angela's answer to Olivia. Change the words in **bold** to the correct pronoun or possessive adjective.

Dear Olivia

I think you should ask Adam why [1]~~**Adam**~~ *he* was in the restaurant with Jodie. You said [2]**the restaurant** was near [3]**Jodie and Adam's** office, so maybe [4]**Jodie** wanted to talk to [5]**Adam** about work. Maybe it was [6]**Jodie's** birthday – or [7]**Jodie and Adam** might just be friends. Just because you saw [8]**Jodie and Adam** together, it doesn't mean [9]**Adam** is going out with [10]**Jodie**. Why don't you talk to Adam and get [11]**Adam's** side of the story before you talk to your sister? Then you can help [12]**Samantha** if there's something wrong in [13]**Samantha's** relationship with Adam.

Angela

5 Read letter C again. Then read Angela's answer to Yvonne. Choose the correct words.

Dear Yvonne

Life is often difficult for married couples when [1]*(they)/them* have [2]*them/their* first child. Why don't [3]*you/your* talk to [4]*you/your* husband and tell [5]*his/him* how [6]*you/your* feel? You say that [7]*he/him* works hard, but Maria's [8]*him/his* baby too. [9]*You/Your* daughter needs to spend time with [10]*she/her* father – it's important for babies to have both parents in [11]*their/them* lives. Tonight why don't you both put Maria to bed? You also say Rick goes out with [12]*him/his* friends every Saturday – maybe you can go out with [13]*you/your* friends on Fridays and [14]*he/his* can be with [15]*him/his* daughter.

Angela

6 **a** Read letter A again. Think of five things Jasper should do to lose weight and why he should do them. Make notes in the table.

advice	**reason why**
eat more salads	they're low in fat

b Imagine you are Angela. Write your advice to Jasper.

- Use your notes from the table in **6a**.
- Use pronouns and possessive adjectives.
- Use *You should …* , *You shouldn't …* and *Why don't you … ?* to give advice.
- Read and check for mistakes.
- Give your advice to your teacher next class.

Tick the things you can do in English in the Reading and Writing Progress Portfolio, p88.

A town by the sea

Reading a tourist brochure; an email
Writing common mistakes; a description of a town or city
Review Present Simple; punctuation

1 **a** Read the tourist brochure about Brighton, a town on the south coast of England. Match places 1–6 to A–F on the map.

1 West Pier	*E*	3 The Esplanade		5 The Lanes	
2 Brighton Pier		4 The Royal Pavilion		6 North Laine	

Things to do in Brighton

The Seafront

The best way to get to know Brighton is to walk along the Esplanade on the seafront. Here you'll see some of the town's most beautiful old buildings. Many of the town's most important tourist attractions* are also close to the seafront, in the area opposite Brighton Pier.

The Piers

Brighton has two piers, West Pier and Brighton Pier. Unfortunately you can't visit West Pier because parts of it fell into the sea in 1987 and in 2003. Brighton Pier is over 100 years old and is very popular with tourists. It's open 364 days a year, from 10 a.m. to midnight. Admission* is free.

The Royal Pavilion

The Royal Pavilion, on Pavilion Parade, is probably the most famous building in Brighton and it was one of King George IV's* palaces in the 19th century. It is open from 9.30 a.m. to 5.45 p.m. April to September and from 10 a.m. to 5.15 p.m. for the rest of the year. Admission is £9.80 for adults and £5.60 for children, or you can buy a family ticket for two adults and two children for £25.20.

**tourist attractions* = places people want to visit when they are on holiday
**admission* = the price to visit this place
**King George IV* = King of Great Britain 1820–1830

The Lanes and North Laine

The small area between North Street and the Esplanade is called The Lanes. This is the best place to go shopping for clothes, or you can just relax in a café and watch the world go by. North Laine, between North Street and Trafalgar Street, is another popular shopping area and prices there are usually cheaper than in The Lanes.

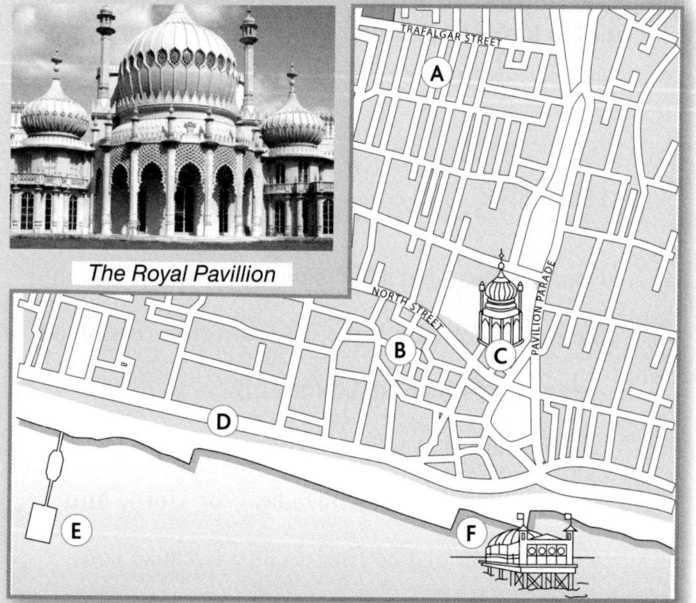

The Royal Pavillion

b Read the information again. Answer these questions.

1 What's the best thing to do when you arrive in Brighton?

Walk along the Esplanade.

2 Which pier can you visit?

3 Do you pay to visit Brighton Pier?

4 Can you visit the Royal Pavilion in December?

5 A mother, father and three children want to visit the Royal Pavilion. How much do they pay?

6 Which place is more expensive to go shopping, The Lanes or North Laine?

2 Read Alejandro's email and tick the places that he went to on the map.

Dear Harriet

How are you? I'm studying English at a language school in Brighton. Is a very good school and the people is very friendly. I study for three hours every morning and I like very much my classes. The name of my teacher is Caroline. She borned in Liverpool, but now she lives in Brighton.

After classes I usually visit places in Brighton with my friend Agnès. She's french, she has 29 years old and she's doctor. Two days ago we went shopping in The Lanes and yesterday night I went to Brighton Pier and had fish and chips! Tomorrow we're going to see the Royal Pavilion. Agnès think Brighton is boring, but I'm not agree with her.

I'm going to stay here for two more weeks. Would you like to visit me.

Love Alejandro

HELP WITH WRITING Common mistakes

3 **a** Students often make these mistakes when they write.

1 capital letters: *She's **I**talian.* not ~~*She's italian*~~.
2 possessive *'s*: *My friend**'s** name is **A**bby.* not ~~*The name of my friend is Abby*~~.
3 *it* as a subject: ***It's** very interesting.* not ~~*Is very interesting*~~.
4 punctuation: *Can you help me**?*** not ~~*Can you help me*~~.
5 *a/an* with jobs: *He's **a** teacher.* not ~~*He's teacher*~~.
6 Present Simple *-s* with *he/she/it*: *He work**s** in London.* not ~~*He work in London*~~.

b Students also often make mistakes with these phrases.

1 *people are* … not ~~*people is*~~ …
2 *I like jazz very much.* not ~~*I like very much jazz*~~.
3 *He was born in London.* not ~~*He borned in London*~~.
4 *I am 26 (years old).* not ~~*I have (26 years old)*~~.
5 *last night.* not ~~*yesterday night*~~.
6 *I don't agree.* not ~~*I'm not agree*~~.

c Read Alejandro's email again. Find the 12 mistakes from **3a** and **3b** and correct them.

4 **a** Imagine you are visiting a friend in a different town or city for the weekend. It's now Saturday evening. Make notes on these things.

the place you're visiting	
where you are staying and people you're staying with	
good/bad things about the place	
three things you did today (Saturday)	
two things you're going to do tomorrow (Sunday)	

b Write an email to someone in your family and tell them about your weekend.

- Use your notes from the table in **4a**.
- Use paragraphs.
- Read and check for the mistakes in **3a** and **3b**.
- Write the email again if you want to.
- Give your email to your teacher next class.

Tick the things you can do in English in the Reading and Writing Progress Portfolio, p88.

At the airport

Reading airport signs; a postcard
Writing useful phrases for a postcard
Review airport vocabulary; verb forms

departure lounge = the place where you wait for your flight
**EU* = European Union

1 **a** Match signs A–E with places 1–5 in an airport.

1 [B] at passport control
2 [ ] at the check-in desk
3 [ ] at the entrance to the departure lounge*
4 [ ] on a public computer
5 [ ] on a public phone

b Read the signs again. Answer these questions.

1 Do you need to pay for all internet sites? *No, you don't.*
2 Where should you put your sharp objects? ______
3 Can you use a credit card to make a phone call? ______
4 Which sign should a Japanese tourist look for at passport control? ______
5 Can you pay for the internet in euros? ______
6 Do you need to show your ticket to go into the departure lounge? ______

2 Look at boards A and B. Which board gives you information about:

1 Planes coming into the airport?
2 Planes leaving the airport?

A

DEPARTURE	FLIGHT	TO	BOARDING	GATE	STATUS
16.15	SK3851	VANCOUVER	15.15	46	GATE CLOSED
16.30	TK1992	ISTANBUL	15.30	52	FINAL CALL
16.35	AA091	CHICAGO	15.35	34	BOARDING
16.35	AA131	NEW YORK	15.35	35	CANCELLED*
16.50	SK506	COPENHAGEN	15.50	59	DELAYED*
17.15	PK788	KARACHI	16.15	49	GO TO GATE

B

ARRIVAL	FLIGHT	FROM	STATUS
16.15	JL401	TOKYO	BAGGAGE* IN HALL
16.25	SK509	OSLO	LANDED
16.40	BT651	RIGA	EXPECTED 16.54
16.55	KE907	SEOUL	EXPECTED 17.25

cancelled = the plane isn't going to fly
delayed = the plane is going to be late
baggage = luggage

3 Look at boards A and B again. Are these sentences true (T) or false (F)?

1 [T] You should go to gate 49 if you're flying to Karachi.
2 [ ] The flight from Seoul is late.
3 [ ] Flight TK1992 to Istanbul is going to leave soon.
4 [ ] The flight from Tokyo hasn't arrived.
5 [ ] Flight SK506 is going to leave on time.
6 [ ] It's too late to get on your plane to Vancouver.
7 [ ] You can fly to New York at 16.35 today.
8 [ ] Flight BT651 is early.
9 [ ] You can get on your plane to Chicago now.

4 Joe is on holiday in the USA. Read the postcard. Are these sentences true (T) or false (F)?

1 [F] Joe spent three days in Boston.
2 [ ] He's staying in New York at the moment.
3 [ ] He travelled to Cape Cod by car.
4 [ ] He went to New York before Cape Cod.
5 [ ] He went whale-watching the day before he wrote the postcard.
6 [ ] He doesn't know anyone in New York.
7 [ ] Ed and Lyn said goodbye to Joe at the airport.

Hi Ed and Lyn
I'm having a wonderful time in the USA!
I spent two days in Boston and then took a boat to Cape Cod. I'm staying in a place called Hyannis – it's an old town on the coast. The weather's good and there's lots to do here.
I went deep-sea fishing on Sunday and yesterday I went on a whale-watching trip. That was fantastic! Tomorrow I'm going to New York to stay with some friends. See you soon!
Love
Joe
PS Thanks for coming to say goodbye at the airport!

Ed & Lyn Lee
23a Moreton Rd
London
N15 6TT
UK

HELP WITH WRITING A postcard

5 **a** We often use these phrases when we write postcards. Fill in the gaps with these words.

~~having~~ going spent See staying weather lots

1 I'm *having* a great/wonderful/fantastic time in (the USA).
2 I ______ (two) days in (Boston).
3 I'm ______ in a place called (Hyannis).
4 The ______'s good/beautiful/terrible.
5 There's ______ to do/see here.
6 I'm ______ to (New York).
7 ______ you soon/in a few days/next week.

b Underline phrases 1–7 in the postcard.

TIP • We use *a place called* … when we think the other person doesn't know this place:
I'm staying in a place called Hyannis. (Joe's friends don't know this place.)
I'm going to New York. (His friends know this place.)

6 **a** Imagine you are on holiday in a place you know. Make notes about these things.

- the place you're staying
- the weather
- places you went to and when you went there
- what you did at these places
- things you're going to do

b Write a postcard to your teacher.

- Use your notes from **6a**.
- Use five or more phrases from **5a** in your postcard.
- Read and check for mistakes.
- Write your teacher's name and the school address on the postcard.
- Send or give your postcard to your teacher.

Tick the things you can do in English in the Reading and Writing Progress Portfolio, p88.

Elementary Reading and Writing Progress Portfolio

Tick the things you can do in English.

Portfolio	Reading	Writing
1 p64	☐ I can understand addresses. ☐ I can understand a hotel registration form.	☐ I can use capital letters. ☐ I can write addresses. ☐ I can fill in a hotel registration form.
2 p66	☐ I can understand short texts about people's possessions.	☐ I can use correct punctuation (full stops, question marks, etc.). ☐ I can write about my possessions.
3 p68	☐ I can understand important information about people's daily lives (job, family, daily routine, free time, etc.).	☐ I can use connecting words like *and*, *but* and *because*. ☐ I can write about my daily life in simple phrases and sentences (job, family, daily routine, free time, etc.).
4 p70	☐ I can find the most important information in adverts for restaurants (opening times, types of food, etc.). ☐ I can understand simple emails.	☐ I can make and respond to suggestions about places to go and where/when to meet. ☐ I can write simple emails to friends.
5 p72	☐ I can understand a story about a past event (a night out, etc.).	☐ I can use paragraphs in a story. ☐ I can use connecting words like *after*, *when* and *and then* to show the order of events. ☐ I can write a simple story about a past event in my life.
6 p74	☐ I can find the most important information in adverts for free time activities, concerts, etc. ☐ I can understand simple text messages.	☐ I can write short simple messages to tell somebody where I am and where to meet.
7 p76	☐ I can find the most important pieces of information in adverts for houses and flats (price, number of rooms, etc.). ☐ I can understand a simple letter to a friend.	☐ I can use paragraphs in a letter. ☐ I can organise a letter correctly (address, date, etc.). ☐ I can write a simple letter to a friend.
8 p78	☐ I can find the most important information in job adverts (type of job, working hours, etc.). ☐ I can understand a simple formal letter.	☐ I can organise a formal letter correctly (address, date, etc.). ☐ I can write a simple formal letter.
9 p80	☐ I can understand simple tourist information (on an internet website, in a tourist brochure, etc.).	☐ I can describe my country with simple words and phrases. ☐ I can use paragraphs in a description of a place.
10 p82	☐ I can understand a simple newspaper article where people ask for advice.	☐ I can use pronouns and possessive adjectives correctly. ☐ I can give advice.
11 p84	☐ I can understand a simple tourist brochure about a town or city.	☐ I can write an email to a friend and describe the place and things I did or I am going to do.
12 p86	☐ I can understand signs, and departure and arrivals boards at an airport. ☐ I can understand short simple messages on postcards.	☐ I can write a postcard to a friend when I am on holiday.